LORI R.
ANDERSON

ANNETTE M.
BESEMAN

GIESLER

ROGERS

WHITAKER

Read, Reflect, and Write To Connect with God

Unleash Your Pen

Minneapolis, Minnesota

Unleash Your Pen: Read, Reflect, and Write To Connect with God
by Lori R. Anderson, Annette M. Beseman,
Janell Giesler, Dawn M. Rogers, and Lori Waite Whitaker

This devotional is published by Minnesota Christian Writers Guild
MNCHRISTIANWRITERS.COM
Cover by Madeline Deckert
Interior design by Jason Sisam

Print ISBN: 979-8-218-67092-4

Printed in the United States
10 9 8 7 6 5 4 3 2 1

Contents

This book is dedicated to God and all who may read it.

Foreword

What a sweet privilege it is to introduce you to the gift you hold in your hands! It is an additional honor for me that these five heart-full women attended one of my "Writing as a Spiritual Practice" workshops several years ago. As I had journaled in my own life, I found it to be a valuable tool for listening to God/Jesus/Holy Spirit speak to me. And as a spiritual director, I have loved sharing this tool with others. I remember these women being in my workshop that day and the blessing it was to see them be inspired to write also. Imagine my delight when I discovered they had formed an ongoing writing group to support one another in this practice. That would have been enough gifts right there, but then they invited me to read their manuscript and offer my introduction here. I am so grateful.

The meditations and writings you are holding in your hand right now are a precious collection of forty faith/life stories. Each of these women have shared their honest journey of faith as they wrote, prayed, and dealt with the realities of life's struggle with family, work, and just being. They deal also with the heart-wrenching grief of losing loved ones and the blessing of the Holy Spirit's presence through all of it. Each entry of theirs leans into a message from scripture as it applies to their own circumstances and thoughts. Then each writer ends with an invitation for you to write your own thoughts and prayers.

As I read these meditations, I was moved by how each woman lets God's Word fall on their heart and writes such tender and inspiring thoughts as they prayed and lived into the truth of God's Word and their own personal journeys.

It is my prayer and hope that you too will be inspired and allow yourself to respond to the invitation to "unleash your pen." I pray you too will find God's loving presence and guidance as you allow yourself to write about the struggle and the truth of your own faith journey. You are holding an amazing gift of inspiration! May you be encouraged in your faith as you ponder God's words, their words, and your own words!

With gratitude,
Julie A. Bonde
Spiritual Director, Workshop Facilitator, Teacher, Writer,
Photographer, Mother, Grandmother
Whispersofwisdom.biz

Introduction

In November 2021, when COVID was still reorienting our lives, the five of us were part of a group of women who joined a Zoom workshop called *Writing as a Spiritual Practice*, presented by Julie Bonde of Christos Center for Spiritual Formation in Lino Lakes, Minnesota. Two loves drew each of us to the class —the love of Jesus with a deep desire to grow closer to him, and the love of writing and desire to develop this creative outlet to process our lives.

We spent the day writing in response to prompts that utilized several writing methods including lists, poems, free verse, and essays. As we responded to each prompt, we shared with one another what we had written. It was encouraging to both the writer and the listener. The presenter introduced us to the concept of a writing group—a group of people meeting regularly to write together and share with each other.

As the workshop ended, several of us wanted to continue to experience this new-found way to connect with Jesus through our love of writing and to stay connected with each other. We asked the presenter how to join a writing group. Her response: "Start one!" The five of us did just that. Our writing group has been meeting twice a month for more than three years. We are geographically scattered, so we continue to meet by Zoom. We have come to view writing as a precious gift God imparted to each of us. Sharing our writings within our group has become a way to both encourage one another in the practice of writing and develop Christian community as we process together what is happening in our lives based on what is revealed in our writing.

By way of introduction of each author, we each would like to share what this writing group has meant to us.

As our group began to meet, joys and sorrows, prayer requests, encouragement, and helpful feedback were shared as the group morphed into a spiritual direction writing group of sorts. Throughout our time together, we have walked through illnesses and deaths of parents, struggled through the challenges of family relationships, welcomed grandchildren, and become dear friends. This gave us plenty of fodder to reflect on God's presence and faithfulness in our lives through it all, some of which is reflected in the book you hold in your hands. We treasure and affirm each other's many gifts, and I am blessed to be part of this wonderful group!

— *LORI ANDERSON*

I never dreamed that attending the workshop would motivate my desire to write the way it has. I have pondered and written responses to prompts that I may never have thought about, uncovering things deep inside. A hidden desire to write what I've had in my heart for years has bloomed! This group has been a safe place to share what I have written and has given me courage to experiment with poetry and other forms of writing. I have been excited to share my writing with friends. What a joy to discover that I do have a creative side! I have learned how writing provides a special connection to God—allowing me to use a skill with which he has uniquely gifted me. I can process my spiritual journey, sometimes even preaching to myself through my own written words.

— *ANNETTE BESEMAN*

Our writing group started as God's invitation for me to participate in a season of fellowship with women of like mind and like heart. God promises where two or three gather in his name, he will be present, and so we have faithfully gathered in God's presence to share our love of devotional writing. We have written our stories and listened to each other's stories. As we participated in this time of shared writing, God wove our individual stories into his greater story of love and grace. I have been strengthened in faith and hope through the spiritual practices of writing, fellowship, and creating together. To God be the glory!

— *JANELL GIESLER*

This writing group has been a consistent and uplifting part of my writing and healing journey. We formed five years after I tragically lost my 15-year-old daughter, Oliva, to suicide. Gathering with these lovely, godly women who share a passion for writing has inspired and encouraged me to grow spiritually, emotionally, and creatively. This group has been a safe and uplifting community where I can share my heart.

As time passed, I began to write about Olivia and my journey after her loss—a process that was both painful and healing. Through it all, this group has surrounded me with patience, grace, hope, love, and steadfast prayer support. Their encouragement has not only helped me heal but also deepened my faith and inspired me to continue sharing my story as a public speaker, emcee, and podcaster. Whether on stage or behind the microphone, I weave threads of my story into my work, relating to others with authenticity and compassion.

— *DAWN ROGERS*

I have journaled personally and shared my life experiences with others through conversation. The opportunity to share my writing with this group has been a delight. The encouragement they have shared has been inspiring. I have felt embraced and accepted by their feedback, providing me a new opportunity to share both my life and writing in an amazing community of friends!

— *LORI WAITE WHITAKER*

After several months of sharing, growing in spiritual friendship and devotion to God, we felt called to share our writings beyond our writing group. After many sessions, we had accumulated a hope chest filled with written treasures. Others could benefit from the delight we experienced. This book reflects each woman's story and the story of this group.

Each daily devotion comes from the response to a writing prompt used in one of our meetings. Each one includes a theme Bible verse, devotion, prayer, and writing prompt. They will encourage and challenge you to explore each topic *and* give you an opportunity to unleash your own pen and write for yourself. Our deep hope is that you will experience the double blessing of growing in relationship with Jesus and unearthing your creativity as you unleash your pen. You may even be inspired to start your own writing group!

Unleash
Your Pen

Lori Anderson

After a long career as a registered nurse in a variety of positions, including faith community nursing, Lori Anderson went back to school for her Master of Science in Nursing degree to become a nurse educator. She is currently an Assistant Professor of Nursing at the University of Northwestern St. Paul School of Nursing in Roseville, Minnesota, where she has been teaching Community and Public Health Nursing for the past ten years. Lori has been married to Bryan for 40 years, has two sons, two daughters-in-love, and four grandchildren aged three and under. A voracious reader and writer who has shelves of unpublished journals about daily family life and camping trips, Lori has always wanted to take her journal writing to the next level. Besides books, she enjoys coffee with friends, walking in nature, camping, gardening, and biking with her husband. Lori and her husband direct the prayer team at their church and live in Lino Lakes, Minnesota.

You can contact Lori at andersonlori24@gmail.com.

Ancient Pathways

 Stand by the roads, and look, and ask for the ancient paths, where the good way is; and walk in it, and find rest for your souls.

— JEREMIAH 6:16 (ESV)

Have you ever rediscovered a special place that immediately brings you back to a precious time you spent there with someone whom you love? As you occupy this space once again, can you almost relive that special time in your mind? Spending time with the Lord, walking on selected paths in several favorite places I routinely visit, brings me back to sacred times spent walking and praying throughout the seasons each year.

Scripture is replete with stories of walking on paths throughout Israel. Both places and spaces captured significant moments with Jesus for the disciples. The Israelites walked in the desert for 40 years. Jesus and the disciples walked through

Galilee in the gospels and the apostles walked on the road to Emmaus after Jesus' resurrection.

I invite you to journey with me as I trace three current paths that help me connect with God. The first path I refer to as a *Sacred Pathway* is near my home providing wooded trails for daily walks. Here I lift up in prayer my family, personal and work concerns, praises, confession and thanks to God. My prayers gain cadence and momentum when my feet plod the path as I immerse myself in nature. For me, prayers often flow more easily when my feet are moving than they do when I am seated in my devotional chair.

My second path is next to our seasonal campground and I call it my *Sanctuary*. This path provides a web of forested trails for hiking. Our campsite is nestled against a wooded backdrop at the trailhead. Here I can walk through sandy trails that wind through forests of pine and hardwood trees, around three meadows and next to a small lake. A parade of seasonal wild-flowers and berries populate the changing landscape that provides this sanctuary for me.

The third pathway is located further away, in our favorite campground in northern Minnesota. More of a place than a path, the space is smaller. Towering pine trees frame a beautiful backdrop to the lake where we have enjoyed many sunsets through decades of family camping. The fading sunlight illuminates the pine needles on the forest floor. A bench and a picnic table near the lakeside complete the space that I call my *Cathedral*.

Having a space or a place to meet with God to walk or just reflect, connects me to my biblical ancestors. They also walked out those ancient paths with God that Jeremiah speaks of, but here the Israelites chose not to walk in the good way. As humans walk these paths throughout time, each of us must make a choice to walk in the good way on the path of life, or not. I continue to hold dear these sacred spaces that nourish my own relationship with God as my walking sanctuaries envelop me in God's presence, and as I choose to walk in the good paths God lays out for me.

PRAYER

Lord, may I find the good way and walk in your ancient paths. Thank you for the beautiful spaces you provide in different spheres of my life that connect me to you. Amen.

UNLEASH YOUR PEN

Reflect on the spaces you have met with God to pray or to bask in his presence. Name those spaces and write about them, offering a prayer of thanks to him.

Be Still...

> Be still, and know that I am God. I will be exalted among the nations, I will be exalted in the earth! The LORD of hosts is with us; the God of Jacob is our fortress.
>
> — PSALM 46:10-11 (ESV)

...IN THE MORNING

"Be still my soul," I prayed. My feet moved even as my soul quieted itself. I walked my path daily from the end of my street, behind nearby neighborhoods, past a community garden plot, a playground, and a ballpark. The path outlined a meadow and gave me options to stay on the paved path or follow a wooded one meandering around a lake. I chose the wooded path. Stately oaks, fallen limbs, abundant underbrush, and flowers greeted me amidst the welcome scent of moist earth. Birds called, and a gentle breeze caressed my face as I sank into this sacred space.

If you saw my path, you wouldn't find it unusual in any way, but it is sacred to me because I meet God here in every season, enjoying the fresh bloom of spring, the wild raspberries in the summer, the falling leaves in autumn, and the stunning winter wonderland after a fresh snowfall. God spoke words of insight and wisdom to me as my feet stepped over fallen logs or followed the twists and turns of the path as I drank in the current seasonal delights each day.

On this path, I pray and praise, lifting my thoughts to Jesus and asking him to meet me. At times, insights come, and I have learned to capture them. I prayed a simple prayer to see something I hadn't seen for a while—an animal or something new.

On my return route, a lone turkey crossed the trail twenty feet in front of me. A few steps further down the path, as I rounded a large sand pile, a deer stood across the ball field next to the wooded area. He stood still for a few minutes and watched me move to the other side, a safer distance away. Then he slipped back into the woods just as a rabbit scampered across my path.

I marveled that Jesus gave me more than I asked for. He sent three animals instead of the one requested. God lavished his love on me that day. It got me thinking about how often I live below his promises, his gifts, and his treasures for me. I don't claim all that is mine in the Lord and fail to grasp the depth of his love and his goodness. God's response to my animal request was a gentle example of his faithfulness. If you ask, you can experience his presence in the stillness of the morning.

...IN THE EVENING

Early evening, and the day is done
Watching now for the waning sun
Quiet my soul after the evening meal
Time for me to relax and heal
Savoring the scent of the crabapple blooms
Marinating in the beauty of my outdoor rooms
Birds fly in for their final feeding
Their songs tell me it's time for breeding
A soft breeze blows as the sun recedes
The whole neighborhood concedes
The crickets now begin their song
Joining in with the heavenly throng
The one who created all you see, hear and smell
"Through all my creatures now to tell
Be still and soak in the beauty I have created for you"

PRAYER

Dear God, I thank you for the simple pleasures and beauty of life all around me, especially in this ever-darkening world. Create in me a spirit of expectancy and wonder. Help me to remember to ask you to show me what I need to see each day that reminds me of your created beauty all around me. In Jesus' name, Amen.

UNLEASH YOUR PEN

Read Psalm 46:10-11 aloud several times. Spend a few minutes thinking about ways you can still your soul in the morning or the evening each day. Jot down your ideas and put one of them into practice today.

Springtime for My Soul

> I will make them and the places surrounding my hill a blessing. I will send down showers in season; there will be showers of blessing.

> — ISAIAH 43:19 (NIV)

A recent Minnesota spring brought snowy March weather in April starting with six inches of snow, followed by three days of summer-like temperatures a week or so later. Lots of rain, thunder, lightning, hail, wind, and cresting rivers, as winter loosened its grip and gave way to spring. A weather free-for-all!

The growing pains of seasonal shifts and transitions are also reflected in the seasons of our lives. My soul begins to open up when our Minnesota winter recedes. I can feel my soul growing along with the expansion of living space, as I rediscover my porch, deck, yard, and garden deserted all winter long. And there's something therapeutic about opening all the windows and scrubbing the house from top to bottom that is good for my soul! Perhaps my soul needs some spiritual spring cleaning, too.

May is the golden month for gardeners when the soil softens, the sun warms, and the days become longer. Garden centers pop up and lure in winter-weary gardeners, with their fresh greenery and bright colors providing a feast for the senses. I've been known to wander the aisles of my favorite garden centers the moment they open just to inhale the smell of dirt and flowers. It's an infusion of spring for my eyes and nose.

Spring flowers are my favorites, because they are the first ones to appear after a long, gray winter. Daffodils, crocuses, and hyacinths poke up from the dead cold earth. Spikes from peonies spring forth, and then wild violets, followed by the bleeding hearts and lilacs.

Honestly, if someone could find a way for lilacs to bloom all summer, that would be heavenly. Lilacs mean spring to me. Growing up, we had lilac bushes at the edge of our garden. My mom would cut an armful of lilacs and put them in a heavy crystal vase reserved only for those flowers. Perched atop our upright piano in the living room, their scent permeated the entire house!

After purchasing my own home, lilac bushes went in early. I now have French, common, and white lilacs. When they bloom, I have vases of them on all levels of my house. I love to share bouquets with my family and neighbors. Lilacs bloom around Mother's Day and last up to two weeks, depending on the season. When they're gone, I grieve for a while, then cut them back so more will appear next spring.

I see God's beautiful creation as flowers emerge from winter's death. He shows us the newness of life with shapes, colors, and scents. This gives us just a taste of his creativity and encourages us to worship him.

The beauty of God's creation is unlimited! Far beyond what we can imagine.

Spring flowers come early and stay for such a short time. Our response should be to delight and savor their presence. Every year I remind myself I should take the entire month of May off from work and focus on the earth springing back to life, noticing new growth on my daily walks.

Spring offers a new beginning. As we reflect on the resurrection of Jesus and the new life he offers us, how can we bring new insights from the Bible with connections from the natural world?

Just as our bodies and minds open to welcome spring, so do our souls! As the seasons change and bring new life, it is natural to take stock of tired winter routines and embrace new spring patterns. Spending more time outside and reintroducing ourselves to our neighbors after a winter of isolation also expands our souls. Join me in savoring the beauty of God's world coming back to life!

PRAYER

Dear Lord, thank you for the freshness and beauty of spring. As I see new life come forth in the physical world, renew my spiritual life with the truth of your resurrection that grants each of us new life. Amen.

UNLEASH YOUR PEN

How can you spring-clean your soul with new routines during this seasonal transition? Are there new habits or patterns you want to embrace, or a scripture verse to memorize? Journal your thoughts and lift up a prayer to the Lord.

The Patchwork Quilt of Life

> You hem me in, behind and before, and lay your
> hand upon me. Such knowledge is too wonderful
> for me; it is high; I cannot attain it.

— PSALM 139:5-6 (ESV)

Patches of quilt pieces describe my current season of life, including teaching, writing, grand-parenting, gardening, and camping. Psalm 139 offers a beautiful description of the depth of God's love and care for me as he hems me in and lays his hand upon me.

The summer season finds me embracing grandchildren and nursing students, nurturing gardens, sewing patches of gardens, writing, and camping into the quilt of my life. While this season of life is particularly pleasant and challenging, painful times come and go as well, representing the underside of my quilt with its knots and threads; a necessary part of the process that allows the beauty of the top side of the quilt of life to show.

Make no mistake, I've experienced the difficult seasons, but as summer begins, I'm rejoicing in this rich and colorful season! I spend my days with a "patch" of teaching in the morning, caring for granddaughters in the afternoons, attending writing meetings, going on morning and evening garden walks, planting and watering, biking, and camping.

My mornings begin with writing, three pages upon awakening, devotional and prayer time, brief exercise, and a morning walk, depending on the forecast. Upon my return home, I walk through the garden to discover fresh blooms. If I have been at school or caring for a granddaughter that day, I come home, change clothes, and go for a garden walk to see how my flower gardens have fared throughout the day. What needs watering, weeding, picking or dead-heading? What has grown or opened since my last garden walk?

Spending time with different patches of a quilt requires organization. I have bags for each one. For example, my "grandma" bag is brightly colored and holds board books, toys, and a variety of toddler-friendly treats; a roller bag holds my teaching supplies. Next comes what my husband refers to as a "life" bag, which includes my Bible, devotional books, writing materials, and books I am reading. It is a must for every camping trip!

Reflecting on the current quilt pattern and bag assortment that make up my life, I'm in a season of deep gratitude and blessing. The pieces of my life mesh together as I nurture grandchildren, future nurses, and gardens to point to the Creator and sustainer of life, the giver of all good things, our life-giving God. In each season, I cultivate faithfulness, gentleness, kindness, and joy with those in my current patches. I celebrate times of plenty, trusting God's unwavering presence through all of life's changing seasons.

God is by my side, working on the myriad of details that make up my life. He is the Lord of the patchwork quilt of my life and yes, Lord of the bags and their contents, too!

PRAYER

Dear Lord, you hold the stitches of our lives within your sovereign plan. You see the pattern of the quilt that represents our lives. Sometimes, the patches make sense, and at other times they may not, but I choose to trust you in all the quilt patches and bags that make up my life. Amen.

UNLEASH YOUR PEN

Consider your current season of life, both life-giving and challenging. Journal about the patches and stitches that God is calling forth in your particular season of life, and lift a prayer of gratitude or petition for help to the one who sustains you in all seasons.

Midweek Snow Sabbath

> The LORD will continually guide you, and satisfy your desire in scorched places, and give strength to your bones; and you will be like a watered garden, and like a spring of water whose waters do not fail.
>
> — ISAIAH 58:11 (NASB)

A three-day snowstorm was predicted, causing a two-day school closure, and canceling both my husband's bus-driving schedule and my classes at the Christian university where I teach. Two unexpected snow days appeared as a midweek gift of time together.

We began the first day with a leisurely brunch, then connected with family and friends to share the good news of my negative biopsy results following a minor surgery two days prior. Day one of our midweek Sabbath landed on Ash

Wednesday, giving me extra time to savor the devotional readings I chose to follow for the season of Lent. After clearing our driveway, my husband made a roaring fire in our wood stove, and we enjoyed reading biographies in front of the fire in the middle of the day! Following a traditional mid-afternoon Scandinavian tea and a treat time called *fika*, I puttered in my office while listening to a favorite radio host.

That afternoon, we strapped on our cross-country skis for the first time of the season, forging a path through our neighborhood park across piles of pristine snow.

Fresh snow is a picture of dazzling purity, reminding me of God's peace and holiness. I thought of his grace and beauty as our skis sliced through the fresh snow. Nature always provides a welcome time for reflection and prayer in God's created world. So much to thank him for on this day! Back home, we enjoyed lasagna dropped off by our daughter-in-law the day before and watched our favorite TV shows while the fire kept us warm.

That day was a sheer gift from God's hand, full of my favorite things—time with my husband, being in nature, connecting with family and friends, reading by the fire, enjoying tea time, and good food, followed by the great news of negative biopsy results! God's love for me felt like a thick, warm blanket, arriving like a shower of unexpected blessings within a single day. I hurried to capture the beautiful essence of that snowy Sabbath in my journal so I would not forget the deep blessings of God.

PRAYER

Dear Heavenly Father, I praise you for the unexpected blessings of life, often wrapped in circumstances I did not plan. Thank you for capturing my attention with your good gifts and the reminder that you delight in granting good things to your children. Amen.

UNLEASH YOUR PEN

Consider the last time your plans were interrupted by an unexpected gift of time or an unanticipated blessing. Lift a prayer of thanks to God for showering you with his love, or journal your thanks to him.

Present in Every Season

> For everything there is a season, and a time for every matter under heaven.
>
> — ECCLESIASTES 3:1 (ESV)

I anticipate the changing seasons with a mix of welcome and resistance. This is especially true as summer gives way to fall, then winter. Spring and summer seasons seem so open, alive with activity, with ease of movement in and out of the house due to predominantly pleasant weather. I find myself making more of an effort to adjust to the changes with intentionality, rather than letting them carry me along until I'm surprised by the date on the calendar.

On a walk one day, this analogy came to me: My soul is like a taco! In spring and summer, my soul feels like a taco salad—open, full of color, and delicious. In the fall, my soul feels a bit more like a hard-shell taco, with outside edges protecting what is inside from the cold, wind, rain, and especially the dark, but still with good things inside.

Come winter, I'm more like a soft-shell taco, all rolled up within myself, with nourishment on the inside and all cuddled up to practice the Danish tradition of *hygge* that includes candlelight and cozy winter rhythms. Every season has its gifts, from the warmth and light of spring and summer to the cool, cozy days of fall, to the silence and solitude of winter. All of the seasons work on our souls in different ways.

God created the seasons for us to enjoy. In the Midwest, where I live, there is something to celebrate about each season, corresponding with spiritual life. Spring brings resurrection and new life as we celebrate Easter and begin the gardening season. Summer slows our pace and connects us with family and friends outside as we watch our gardens mature. Spiritually, it is a season of abundance and growth.

Fall is a season of letting go of summer's freedom as we embrace routine, welcome the harvest from our gardens, and marvel at the changing leaves. Spiritually, it is a time of celebration and abundance, and of letting go. Winter offers a striking and lonely beauty as we, along with our gardens, are restored below the surface of the frozen land. By quiet reflection on God's Word on bleak winter days, my soul grows beneath the frozen surface of the outside world. By March, how tired I am of the bare black trees and white snow and sky. No color in sight, I am being shaped from within for each season ahead as I faithfully practice time with God and his Word.

With each passing year, I dread the shorter days as summer gives way to fall, and we change our clocks, knowing in the thick of it, that driving to and from work in December will be dark both ways. It almost seems like my soul begins to fold inward, knowing more time is soon spent at hearth and home. As an introvert, I welcome that, yet the greater span of darkness and receding light cast fear into my soul.

When the weather gets colder, the mere act of going outside requires more thought and layers. Daily walks move from early morning to high noon when the sun is warmest, or at least by late afternoon, depending on the day's schedule. And square-foot living space shrinks when the garden and yard are put to bed for the winter. The porch and deck also go into hibernation.

In the last few years, I've elevated seasonal traditions of decorating the house and yard to practice some rituals that help me frame and celebrate the seasons. From candles, afternoon tea, and soft music in the dark evening months to embracing the church year and celebrating Advent with a playlist for my daily walks and special devotional readings. These practices help me celebrate each season more deeply by being aware of the gifts they offer.

Back to the taco analogy: The taco seasoning may be mild or stronger depending on the present season. I know that God is present in every season, even though it may be harder for me to hear his voice in January than it is in June! God speaks to me in different ways through the changing seasons he has created.

PRAYER

Heavenly Father, you created the seasons for me to enjoy. Help me to receive the insights you offer and celebrate the gifts in each of the changing seasons. Amen.

UNLEASH YOUR PEN

Write about how you embrace and celebrate each season where you live. Describe how your spiritual life correlates with each season. What might God be teaching you from this?

Enduring Seasons of Change

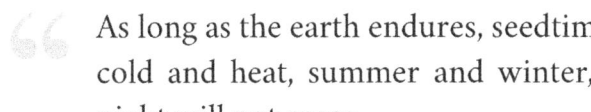

> As long as the earth endures, seedtime and harvest, cold and heat, summer and winter, and day and night will not cease.
>
> — GENESIS 8:22 (CSB)

I'm never ready for the subtle reminders of changing seasons. I love each one and revel in the fact that where I live, we enjoy four distinct seasons. But when I turn the calendar page from July to August, it's as if August holds summer in one hand and fall in the other.

Every year, when August rolls around, my spirit tightens. Summer is on the wane! What happened? Where I live, summer in August equates to ripening garden produce, a rush for back-to-school supplies, and a mad dash to squeeze in one last family vacation up north. Small town festivals abound, celebrating everything from okra to garden harvests. The state fair looms near the end of August—our state's last collective hurrah of summer before school and work calendars again define our days. The dog days of summer mean heat and humidity, with algae on the lakes and ponds as summer simmers down, embracing a transition mode.

I dread August because it's the beginning of summer's end. My heart sinks at the first sign of goldenrod and the subtle ripening of the sumac cones. Fall is on the horizon. I like Autumn very much—once it's officially here. I'm happy in October, the golden month of fall when leaves are at their peak of beauty, days are shorter and cooler, and pumpkin spice abounds.

But not in August.

In August, I am breathless as I think of all I want to do even as the fall schedule demands planning and attention. The sun sets earlier in August. The bright green leaves of May and June turn a faded green, and grasses showcase brown hues. Creation is screaming, "Summer is on its way out. Hurry up and get ready for fall!"

Growing up, August meant shopping for back-to-school clothes, maybe a new book bag or lunch box. There weren't long lists of supplies to buy for classes. Perhaps my dread of August represents lingering childhood grief over the end of *Those Lazy, Hazy, Crazy Days of Summer* as Nat King Cole used to sing on my dad's radio.

While the sunsets come earlier, warm days and cool nights seem to wrestle one another as summer relents and fall officially begins. Once the calendar reaches mid-September, I find myself taking a deep breath as I begin to settle into the regular routines of the school year.

Just as the physical seasons change around me, I'm

reminded that my life with Jesus goes through spiritual seasons of change. Budding and blossoming at times, dropping leaves and going dormant for a time, then springing to life again. Genesis 8:21-22 reflect God's promise to Noah that he will never again curse the ground or "strike down every living creature as I have done." He reminds us that the seasons will come and go as long as the earth remains. No matter what season I am in, I can find enduring hope in the one who created me and the seasons I experience here on earth.

PRAYER

Heavenly Father, thank you for creating changing beauty all around me as one season marches into the next. Thank you for reminding me through your Word that you are my hope in all seasons of life, even when I struggle through the seasonal transitions. In Jesus' name, Amen.

UNLEASH YOUR PEN

Take a few minutes to journal about the current physical and spiritual seasons you are experiencing. Spend time thanking God for the blessings in each season. Pray for his hope and help during challenging seasonal transitions.

Building a Lasting Legacy

 Let us run with endurance the race that is set before us, looking to Jesus, the founder and perfecter of our faith.

— HEBREWS 12:1B-2A (ESV)

As new grandparents, reflecting on the legacy we want to leave to our children and grandchildren consumes our recent thoughts and prayers. Family camping trips offer many tangible ways to pass on a family legacy of faith. Our camping style connects with six foundational values we want to pass on to our loved ones, so this experience packs a powerful investment into the legacy we want to leave behind.

The first foundational value is *faith*. Our camping experiences create a natural space for conversations about God, how we can thank him for his blessings, and the beauty of nature. Our favorite camping spots have small churches nearby where

49

we can worship and make that a tradition. There is prayer before meals and at the evening campfires to thank God for his blessings or to lift a family member in prayer. Weaving prayer throughout the day models its importance to younger watching eyes.

The next value is *family*. My husband and I come from a line of godly generations. While neither of us grew up camping, our family now spends time together in nature, following camping routines and traditions among cousins, aunts and uncles, parents, and grandparents. For example, as soon as we arrive at the campsite, we seem to slip into our own familiar family vernacular that includes memories, jokes, and stories unique to us. Recently, our grandchildren had fun sleeping in the camper or tent, playing with their cousins, and attending the annual family camping fish fry in their tiny camp chairs. They learned to throw rocks into the lake, watch sunsets, and walk to the ice cream shop nearby, a family tradition. The evenings end around a campfire with grandchildren falling asleep on a family member's lap.

The third foundational value is *fun*, with swimming, fishing, and tubing among our favorites. Our boys have a vivid memory of a bird pooping on my hair as he flew over us on a camping trip one year. Another time, a squirrel's nest with baby squirrels dropped from a tree branch onto our screened tent while I was making pancakes. Park ranger to the rescue!

Food is the fourth foundation. The Anderson family loves to eat. My husband takes the lead with menu planning, shopping and preparation.

I am blessed!

When camping, we have a fish fry complete with my corn

chowder, my sister-in-law's zucchini surprise, and other delights.

A fifth foundation is *flora* (plants of a particular region) and *fauna* (the animals of a particular region). We have God's creation all around us and can marvel at the loon's call, the beauty of a sunset, and the woods around our campsite. My family loves to fish and explore the lake looking for bald eagles, loons, and God's beauty all around us. This year, I found wild, ripe blueberries in the campground and picked a quart of them.

The sixth foundation is *finances*. We Andersons are thrifty. My husband taught me this skill, and we are always looking for deals in the thrift shops near the campground. I'll always cherish the look of pure joy on my husband's face when he received his senior pass for national park campgrounds at 62. There couldn't be a better gift. The card slashed our camping fee in half, enabling us to camp for $14 per night.

Our family works to weave these foundational principles into other seasons of our lives as well. With God's wisdom and guidance, we continue to run the race with endurance, and looking to Jesus, the founder and perfecter of our faith. We pray for our children and grandchildren and work to lead by example as God empowers us. It is a joy to welcome our sons and their young families on our camping trips as we inspire the next generation to love God, family, nature, food, flora, fauna, and fun in the great outdoors.

PRAYER

Heavenly Father, thank you for the gifts of faith, family, and the beauty of nature that you created for us to enjoy! Your presence in each of these gifts demonstrates the love you have for each of us. Help us to share that love well with the next generation. Amen.

UNLEASH YOUR PEN

Reflect on the blessings of your family legacy. Give thanks and bring to God the parts that are painful and need healing. Start right where you are, and with God's help, you can create your unique legacy of faith for those you love.

Annette Beseman

Annette is single and retired, living in Minneapolis, Minnesota. After working in various disciplines in a medical device company, she spent the last 26 years of her career as Director of Administration in her home church. She enjoyed applying her administrative gifts in church and ministry. The joy of retirement has been being available to care for and spend time with the people God has placed in her life including her elderly parents, her nieces, nephews and greats, friends, and mentees. She has employed journaling in her daily devotional time for years to pray and process her thoughts with Jesus. In addition to writing, she enjoys reading, music, cooking, Bible studies, traveling, and being part of her church community.

You can contact Annette at abeseman@comcast.net.

God's Peace Transcends

> Peace I leave with you. My peace I give to you. I do not give to you as the world gives. Don't let your heart be troubled or fearful.

— JOHN 14:27 (CSB)

I look out my window this evening, and everything looks quiet and still. The pond is frozen. There is no movement. As the sun sets, just a red glow remains. Cozy lights adorn the windows of homes across the pond. It feels like peace. Yet my awareness of what's happening in the world tells me something different—something opposite of peace. Noise, stress, war, dying, political upheaval. Perhaps those cozy lights aren't cozy at all. Perhaps they're masking discord, chaos, or worse.

The reality is, there has not been peace in our world since Adam and Eve bit into the forbidden fruit. Yet, Jesus says,

"Peace I leave with you. My peace I give to you. I do not give to you as the world gives." The prophecy of Isaiah calls Jesus the prince of peace. How is his peace different than the world's peace?

The world defines peace in terms of circumstances, as an absence of trouble, war, or disagreements. But this quest for worldly peace, however noble, quickly dissolves into a hopeless pursuit. It will not happen on this side of heaven as long as we sinners inhabit the planet.

Jesus, however, defines peace in terms of relationship—our relationship with God. Jesus himself is our peace, having died to bridge the gap between our sin and God's love and grace. Our reconciliation through Jesus Christ means that by the Holy Spirit living in us, we can experience true peace even as the lack of it swirls around us in the world. It's hard to comprehend, and even the apostle Paul tells us that the "peace of God transcends all understanding" (Philippians 4:7). Claiming the peace that comes as a gift from Jesus will "guard our hearts and minds in Christ Jesus." It will settle our souls amidst worldly chaos.

We experience more and more of this gift of peace as we walk with Jesus, learning to trust him in every situation. Romans 15:13 says, "May the God of hope give you all joy and peace, *as you trust in him.*" Growing our trust in God will not be a worthless pursuit. It brings us hope, joy and peace.

PRAYER

Dear Jesus, thank you today for your gift of peace that transcends understanding. Help me to lay my worldly concerns at your feet, and to trust in you to carry me through. Help me to lay claim to your perfect peace today and to share it with others. Amen.

UNLEASH YOUR PEN

How have you experienced the peace of Jesus amidst worldly concerns? How can you transform your worries into trust in Jesus?

My Imperfect Heart

— PROVERBS 4:23 (NIV)

Valentine's Day had just passed, and the leader of my writing group suggested we each draw a picture of what our heart looks like. She asked, "What is in your heart? Who is in your heart? What words are in your heart?" After drawing our picture, we were to write about whatever came out in the drawing.

I got out my colored pencils and started filling the heart on the page with colorful words. These were positive words like gratitude, family, faith, and love. The heart was almost filled and then I began to think of other, less positive, aspects of my heart. I picked up the black pencil and started writing words like jealousy, idolatry, and impatience. I discovered there was a little pocket of my heart that was dark and hidden. But together, it was all in my heart. My imperfect, sacred heart.

This poem arose:

> *Light, and a pocket of dark*
> *Color, and a pocket of gray*
> *Deep, and a pocket of shallow*
> *Others, and a pocket of self*
> *Gifts, and a pocket of burdens*
> *Free, and a pocket of bondage*
> *Love, and a pocket of indifference*
> *Jesus, and a pocket of flesh*
> *Jesus, fill the pockets with the fruit of your Holy Spirit.*
> *Keep my heart soft to receive your goodness.*
> *Guard my heart, for everything I do flows from it.*

A quick word search of "heart" in the Psalms reveals the complexity of the spiritual human heart. It holds love, joy, gladness, courage, trust, humility, and wisdom. It meditates, celebrates, plans, imagines, and treasures, and it is moved. But the heart also holds deceit, malice, evil, injustice, and arrogance. It goes astray, hates, and hardens. The heart feels anguish, suffering, abuse, dismay, and distress. The heart breaks, gets wounded, races, and shudders.

As the Psalmist says, we must guard our hearts because everything in them informs and directs our lives. With all our hearts we can cry out to God, thank him, seek him, praise him, follow his instructions, and seek his favor. He faithfully responds. He knows our hearts, strengthens our hearts, examines our hearts, instructs our hearts, and creates a clean heart within us.

PRAYER

Dear Lord, thank you for knowing my heart—every pocket of it. Reveal to me what is hidden. Soften what has hardened. Open my heart to you. Amen.

UNLEASH YOUR PEN

Take some time to search your heart. Draw a picture of your heart. What is in your heart? Who is in your heart? What words are in your heart? Inside your heart picture, draw, write words, and include photos or anything else that represents your heart. Once you have completed your heart, spend some time journaling about what your heart looks like. Write a poem, a story, a prayer, a letter, a song, or whatever best describes the condition of your heart.

From Hopelessness to Eternal Hope

> May our Lord Jesus Christ himself and God our Father, who has loved us and given us eternal encouragement and good hope by grace, encourage your hearts and strengthen you in every good work and word.
>
> — 2 THESSALONIANS 2:16-17 (CSB)

One day, as I was going through my morning routine, it suddenly entered my mind that the next time my mother would be able to leave her nursing home would be the day she dies. At 91 years old, she is suffering from dementia and is immobile, making it impossible to take her out of her facility. I don't know why this came to mind so suddenly, but it simultaneously surprised and saddened me. Surprised because though I knew she was unable to leave her facility, I hadn't stopped to consider that this was forever. And sad because this isn't the life I wanted for my mother. On this side of heaven, there is no getting better, I thought. There is no hope. Sometimes, someone else's suffering, as in the case of my mother, becomes your own.

We live in a fallen world—fallen from a place of perfection and paradise to a place of brokenness, chaos, and sin. A world that brings the pressure of minor and major issues and concerns—political divisions, war, family and relationship breakdowns, financial hardship, crime, sexual immorality, and on and on. So many reasons for us to lose hope. We get stuck in this hopeless place, complaining and lamenting.

But...we have Jesus!

If we look to the Word of God, this one sentence in 2 Thessalonians 2:16-17 is packed with the promise of hope and encouragement—both today and eternally—and Jesus Christ is the source of life. By his unconditional love and grace, and by his sacrificial work on the cross, we have hope that we will one day be in a place of perfection—in paradise with him, eternally.

This is good hope.

Jesus sees us. He knows the realities of our sinful, fallen world. He knows that we need encouragement deep in our hearts and encouragement that causes us to look to eternity to give us hope for today. We are strengthened by his promises as we journey through this fallen world, trying our best to make it a better place. As we do, maybe we can encourage someone else's hopeless heart, being the hope-bearer for someone who is no longer capable of understanding eternal hope.

PRAYER

Dear Jesus, thank you for being my good hope, my eternal encouragement, and my strength every day. As I journey through difficult times, help me to live in the light of eternity and turn my hopeless heart toward you. Keep me aware and mindful of those around me who need to be pointed toward your love, grace, and good hope. Amen.

UNLEASH YOUR PEN

Make a list of things that cause you anxiety, stress, or hopelessness. Beside each item, write a word of encouragement as if Jesus were speaking to you. Perhaps choose Bible verses that speak God's truth into your concerns.

Surrender in Stillness

> Be still, and know that I am God; I will be exalted among the nations, I will be exalted in the earth.

— PSALM 46:10 (NIV)

Today as I looked at the large pond in my backyard, it sat still, clear as glass. The surroundings were reflected distinctly in the motionless water. Whenever I look deeply upon God's creation, it brings to mind the lessons he teaches about living and walking with him in this world. I began to ask myself questions. What happens when my body is still, when my soul is still? Does it make things clear? What happens when I am still before the Lord? Does his love, faithfulness, and goodness reflect into my soul?

The passage that always comes to mind when I think of being still is Psalm 46:10: "Be still, and know that I am God." It's important to read this passage in the context of the entire psalm. It is thought that this psalm may have been written by King Hezekiah during the time of God's deliverance of Jerusalem from the Assyrians.[1] It speaks of troubling times with the earth trembling, mountains toppling into the depths of the seas, and water roaring and foaming. It speaks of nations raging and kingdoms falling. Do you ever feel like this could describe the state of our world today with political unrest, war, racial strife, moral decline, culture wars, and more? Or maybe personal trials are rocking your world—a broken relationship, job stress or loss, sickness, or financial issues.

The context of this psalm is what makes the command to "be still, and know that I am God" so compelling, both then and now. What does it mean to "be still?" I think of stillness as silence, calm, and quiet in mind and spirit. But in this context, the meaning is deeper. The Hebrew word for "still" is *raphah*[2], which means to be weak, to let go, to release. Therefore, we should surrender our worries, concerns, and anxieties. Let go of trying to control things. The good news, when we surrender, we are surrendering to God who is sovereign and in control over all. He says, "I will be exalted among the nations. *I* will be exalted in the earth." He is *above* it all!

What does it mean to "know that I am God"? The Hebrew word for "know" is *yada*,[3] which means to perceive, to understand, to discern, to know intimately, as in sexual relations. This is a deep kind of knowing that comes in the context of an intimate relationship. By God's design and invitation, we can know him in this way.

These two commands, "be still" and "know," hinge upon each other. Knowing comes from stillness, in times of honesty, authenticity and vulnerability with God. When you test God by surrendering to him, knowing transforms into trust—trust in the God who knows you, loves you, and holds in the palm of his hand everything that you surrender to him.

PRAYER

Dear Lord, thank you for your precious Word and the invitation to be still and know that you are God. Help me to come to you as my refuge in times of trouble, to surrender my worries and anxieties. You are a great God—greater than any struggle I may face or any calamity this world endures. As I surrender, please grow my trust in you. I want to know you more. Amen.

UNLEASH YOUR PEN

Set aside time to be still. Ask God to bring to mind something that you could surrender. Choose to surrender it to God now. Listen to God. What do you know about God now that you didn't know before you surrendered?

I Know for Sure

> I am persuaded that neither death nor life, nor angels nor rulers, nor things present nor things to come, nor powers, nor height nor depth, nor any other created thing will be able to separate us from the love of God that is in Christ Jesus our Lord.
>
> — ROMANS 8:38-39 (CSB)

There are few things in life that I know for sure:

I know that Jesus loves me...
even when I sin habitually
even when I choose idols over him
even when I give him too low priority
even when I lack trust
even when I worry
even when I fall or fail

even when I am jealous of someone else he created
even when I become frustrated
even when I lack self-control
even when pride rears its ugly head.

Nothing can separate me from the love of Jesus...
because he created me in his image even before I was
conceived
because I am his treasured possession
because his death on the cross paid for my sin; past,
present, and future
because his Holy Spirit lives in me
because his love for me does not depend on me.

These things I know for sure.

PRAYER

Dear Lord, thank you for the assurance of your love for me and that nothing can separate me from you. Remind me of this truth as I live my imperfect life and when I relate with the imperfect lives of others. I love you! Amen.

UNLEASH YOUR PEN

Reflect upon your relationship with Jesus. What do you know for sure about Jesus? Write a prayer of gratitude to him.

Giving Thanks When It's Hard

> Rejoice always, pray constantly, give thanks in everything; for this is God's will for you in Christ Jesus.
>
> — 1 THESSALONIANS 5:16-18 (CSB)

January had just begun, and I'd chosen "pray" as my word for the year. On a January morning, I journaled and prayed, seeking guidance for some of life's difficulties. I asked God to teach me how to be in continual, unceasing communication with him through prayer. This became my heart's desire.

I searched for the word *pray* in my Bible, and God led me to 1 Thessalonians 5:6-18. I resonated with the command to pray constantly. However, the phrase that captivated me was "give thanks in everything."

Everything? Even the hard stuff? Even the things I was trying to pray away?

For years, I've maintained a gratitude journal. Focusing on gratitude has been a wonderful practice; it helps me find the positive, regardless of what's happening. I've always loved this quote by G.K. Chesterton, "Thanks are the highest form of thought, and gratitude is happiness doubled by wonder."[1]

I'm sure my gratitude journals would show nothing but positivity if I reread them. Even in difficult times, I could always find something good for which to give thanks. But I doubt I would find any entries giving thanks for any negative or difficult things I was experiencing. Yet God said, "Give thanks in *everything*."

As I continued to pray and process with God, I heard him begin to explain things to me. To give thanks in everything requires intention; it doesn't happen as naturally as gratitude for the good things. To give thanks in everything requires focus on God, and that requires conversation with him who is greater than any of my difficulties or concerns. Being thankful doesn't require ignoring difficulties, positive thinking alone, or boot-strapping your way through life. Rather, it is a loving invitation from God to draw close to him. It's amazing to know God desires a relationship with us and he wastes nothing, even the difficult things, to engage us.

PRAYER

Dear Lord, thank you that when I pray, you answer. You are a loving teacher, showing me how to do hard things. Give me the ability, by the power of your Holy Spirit in me, to give thanks in all circumstances, especially the hard things. In the process, show me new things about you I've never known before and help me to love you more. Thank you that you are able, and you will. Amen.

UNLEASH YOUR PEN

Write about a time when you found it difficult to give thanks. How did you feel about God in this situation? Did God teach you something new in the struggle?

Lessons From a Maple Tree

We all, who with unveiled faces contemplate the Lord's glory, are being transformed into his image with ever-increasing glory, which comes from the Lord, who is the Spirit.

— 2 CORINTHIANS 3:18 (NIV)

A maple tree,
One small part of God's creation.
A new addition to the yard just four years ago
How fast you have grown.
I have a perfect view from my loft—my quiet place
*   with God—where I contemplate your beauty and*
*   transformation.*

You provide needed shade and enjoyment in the warm
*   summer months.*

Green and full of life as you bask in the sun.
Your leaves distinctively shaped
Clinging tightly to your branches during wind and
*   rain.*

As fall comes, ever so slowly, your leaves bleed red from
*   left to right.*
Your right side resists the change and stays green for as
*   long as it can*
Holding on to summer.

Finally, you surrender completely to fall.
Beauty bursting in a bright and rusty red.
From top to bottom, from left to right.
So beautiful—won't you remain until spring?

But the wind comes.
So many leaves have blown off and lay at your feet.
Now you cling to fall but seem helpless to submit to
*   winter.*

The snow and ice and wind batter your branches
Bending in the wind—stiff and barren.
An occasional frosty white or glistening ice covering
*   reminds me that even in the dead of winter, there is*
*   still beauty.*

Spring always comes as a miracle.
How can you come back to life after a bitter winter?
But slowly, you push out your buds

And soon you are full of green leaves again.
I marvel at how you have grown—imperceptible
*   throughout the year*
Yet striking in spring.

Oh, maple tree
You make the changing of the seasons look easy.
But a closer look reveals the struggle.
Each season hangs on as long as it can until you finally
*   give in to the next.*
Always a slow transition, not a quick change.
That is what makes you beautiful.

Oh, that I might embrace and not resist each season.
Surrender to the next
Resilient
Transforming
With hope.
Growing more beautiful through them all
More at one with the Creator.

PRAYER

Dear Lord, thank you for using your creation to speak to me. You have created a common maple tree with the ability to transform and change, and you have created me for the same. Help me lean into the spiritual seasons and transform my heart to be in alignment with yours. Help me to surrender to you with resilience and hope, trusting in your perfect plan. In Jesus' name, Amen.

UNLEASH YOUR PEN

Consider the many wonders of God's creation. Think of one and ponder the lessons it might teach you. Write about it using a format you may have never tried, such as a poem or prayer.

An Unexpected Answer

> In the morning, LORD, you hear my voice; in the morning I plead my case to you and watch expectantly.
>
> — PSALM 5:3 (CSB)

So often, I have asked God, "Why?" Why are you allowing my aging parents to suffer so many disabilities and losses? Why are you allowing my parents' lives to be prolonged when there is so little quality of life left? And the big question—why don't you just take them home? As I have bombarded God with my *whys*, I've wondered, "Is he getting sick of hearing from me about this? Am I missing what He is trying to teach me through this difficult time with my parents?"

God's answer came to me quite unexpectedly through an article that caught my interest on my Facebook feed by the

Gospel Coalition entitled *Death and Dying: A Catechism for Christians*. The article was formatted in a Q&A fashion. As I scrolled through the 72 questions, I was drawn to the set of questions about physician-assisted death and the value of human life. The authors state, "The logic of physician-assisted death assumes that life has no inherent value apart from the value we find in it, and that suffering has no inherent purpose apart from the purpose we give it. Humans have inherent and unconditional value. We matter because of who we are, not merely because of what we can do. Each of us is worth more than we can imagine. No matter what, it is good that we exist."[1]

This question caught my attention. "What does it say about someone's value if we decide that it is no longer good for them to exist?"

The authors said, "If it is no longer good that someone exist, then they have lost their value." I felt a physical reaction and internal guttural groan as I took in the reality that I had questioned whether it was no longer good for Mom and Dad to exist, that their lives were no longer of value.

I read on to another question. "What does love require of us in our attitude toward the life of our neighbor?"

They answered, "To love our neighbor as ourselves requires that, mindful of their inherent value and unconditional value, we always treasure the existence of our neighbor and show them in word and deed how much they matter. To act in a manner that undermines, forgets or denies the value of their life is to fail to love them."[2]

In all my cries and pleas to God to take my parents to heaven, I realized I carried a burden. I tried to impose my will upon God. It took a lot of energy and drained my spirit. All

God asked of me was to love my parents, to value their existence for as long as he chooses to give them life, and to use the limited time they have left to love and care for them instead of wishing this time away. My parents weren't on my mind as I read the Gospel Coalition article, but God used it to challenge my love for them and reframed my thinking, and perhaps even my own aging journey.

Soon after reading this article, I visited my parents. Both have trouble speaking, but I relaxed and enjoyed sitting together, watching television, and being in one another's presence.

When I left, I hugged and kissed them and said, "I love you."

They both said, "I love you, too."

They have lost the ability to do many things at ages 91 and 96, but they can still say, "I love you." That is something I will miss when they are gone.

Was God getting tired of my whining and questions? Maybe. But I'm glad I kept pressing him. I know he heard and answered me in a way I didn't even know I needed. He didn't change my circumstances, but transformed my thinking, and lovingly told me to let go of the *why* questions I had, learning to wait and trust in him. In doing so, God released me from a burden I didn't realize I carried.

PRAYER

Thank you, Lord, for listening to my cries for help. Thank you for grabbing my attention and reframing my thoughts. Thank you for transforming me. Keep me attentive to what you want to reveal to me. Amen.

UNLEASH YOUR PEN

Describe a time when you distinctly felt God speak to you in prayer. What surprised you?

Janell Giesler

Janell began writing as a spiritual practice after retiring from a 30-year career as a physician. She specialized in child and adolescent psychiatry and loved working with children and hearing their stories. Fulfilling a dream, she bought a harp as a retirement gift for herself and has been taking lessons for five years, playing as a volunteer at a hospital and in a senior living facility. She completed a spiritual-direction training program after retirement and enjoys hearing how God is present in the lives of people. Telling a story through writing and music has become one of her passions. Other passions include walks outside, enjoying nature, Bible studies, cooking, and spending time with family and friends. Janell lives in a rural area and has a volunteer dog-sitting service with her husband.

The Hope Chest of Your Heart

> May the God of hope fill you with all joy and peace as you trust in him, so that you may overflow with hope by the power of the Holy Spirit.

— ROMANS 15:13 (NIV)

When I graduated from high school in 1979, I received from my parents a hope chest, a gift symbolizing a melding of their hopes for me at this threshold place in life and my hopes looking forward. Neither of my parents attended college, so we all planned I would go to college and even medical school. There were hopes of marriage and family. Would I return to the rural area where I had grown up or move to some unknown city? Only God knew.

In the past, hope chests were furniture given to unmarried women and were to be filled with items, such as towels, sheets, and family heirlooms, intended to be used in married life. The chests were made of wood, often cedar, which repels insects and fungus and protects the stored items. After more than 40 years, I still have my hope chest, now filled with winter sweaters. It releases a strong scent when opened, an inviting scent infused with memories.

As I reflect on my hope chest, I consider the word *hope*. Hope can be a noun or verb and has a rich spiritual meaning. It's a word that lingers in my heart. My heart is like the hope chest I received long ago, holding treasures that anticipate the future. According to the Blue Letter Bible, in the NIV translation, the word *hope* appears 167 times in 159 verses and appears most often in the book of Psalms. The Hebrew word for hope is *tiqvâh* and is defined as an expectation, cord or rope. It means to bind or to wait for or upon.[1] Hope binds me to God as I wait upon him with expectation. As I trust in God, I overflow with hope by the power of the Holy Spirit.

God is the source of all hope. He is in control and has a plan for all creation. God's plan isn't seen when we look at the world but is revealed when we look to his Word. His Word describes who he is, what he has done in the past, and what his promises are for the future. We don't hope for what is within our power to accomplish; rather, we hope for what Almighty God can do and promises to do. The power of God mediated through the Holy Spirit becomes our strength and an anchor for our soul. This anchor binds us to God. We are held firmly and steadily as we trust and hope in him.

Hope chests were used to store special treasures for a future relationship with one who would be loved. Matthew 6:19-21 speaks of treasures. It says, "Do not store up for yourselves treasures on earth, where moths and vermin destroy, and where thieves break in and steal. But store up for yourselves treasures in heaven… For where your treasure is, there your heart will be also."

I want to fill the hope chest of my heart with the eternal treasures of heaven.

PRAYER

God of hope, please fill me with all joy and peace as I trust in you. May I overflow with hope by the power of your Holy Spirit. In Jesus' name, Amen.

UNLEASH YOUR PEN

What eternal treasures of heaven will fill the hope chest of your heart?

Unforced Rhythms of Grace

> Are you tired? Worn out? Burned out on religion?
> Come to me. Get away with me and you'll recover
> your life. I'll show you how to take a real rest.
> Walk with me and work with me—watch how I do
> it. Learn the unforced rhythms of grace. I won't lay
> anything heavy or ill-fitting on you. Keep
> company with me and you'll learn to live freely
> and lightly.
>
> — MATTHEW 11:28-30 (MSG)

It is the middle of summer; heat and humidity grip my skin, slow me, and even threaten to shut me down. The Mississippi River flows languidly in front of me as I relax on a swing. Deep, hot breaths create feelings of weakness and faintness. I sink into the swing, my legs feeling like cooked spaghetti noodles as my bones melt. Heavy scents of flowers, mud and decay mingle in the air. Staring unfocused, I am mesmerized by the slow flow of river water. The buzzing of bees and wasps keeps my brain on halfhearted alert. I experience summer feelings of tiredness and laziness. I am not sure I should allow rest to take over the command center of my body and my day. There are things that need to be done, but I don't sense the drive to work that I usually have.

In Matthew 11:28-30, I consider *come to me* to be an invitation from God to learn what "real rest" looks and feels like. I feel confused as the verse speaks of walking, working, watching, and learning. These words sound more active than resting —a seeming paradox. The phrase that shouts to me the loudest is "learn the unforced rhythms of grace." God's rhythms of unforced grace abound throughout nature in ocean waves, tides pulled by the moon, sunrises, sunsets, perennial plants, and seasons of the year. God's grace also abounds within a relationship with Jesus, whose grace enters me and is sufficient for all I encounter in life.

Daydreaming, I imagine a scenario. I am waiting at a dance and feel tired, worn out, and burned out. I am listening as soft music plays. Jesus is present and extends his hand in a gentle offer. I hear a question, "Come?" My eyes meet his, and I accept his invitation. We step away together I walk freely, lightly linked under his arms of strength and support, yoked in an embrace. The percussive beating of the music is rhythmic and strong and stabilizes the melodies that tickle and stir in my heart. I can't dance well, and yet, I am dancing effortlessly, responding to the one who leads and teaches. My mind is content. My heart feels joyful and experiences a peace beyond understanding. Tethered and anchored to Jesus, I dance into and beyond the end of time.

My daydream ends with a smile as I sense my body on the swing again. Back-and-forth movement creates a breeze in this season of summer. I am free and flying in the warm air. My spirit and soul keep company with Jesus as I let go of the world's demands. I wait for him to direct me forward again with a gentle wave of his finger, a wink of his eye, or a smile on his lips. Grace abounds in unforced rhythms as I rest and sing softly on this hot summer day.

PRAYER

Jesus, I come to you desiring real rest and wanting to learn unforced rhythms of grace from you. Hold me in relationship with you today and forever so I may live freely and lightly. Thank you, Jesus, Amen.

UNLEASH YOUR PEN

Keep company with Jesus. Watch him. Learn from him. What could unforced rhythms of grace look like in your life today? Write about this.

Who Will Go for Us?

> I heard the voice of the LORD saying, "Whom shall
> I send? And who will go for us?"

— ISAIAH 6:8 (NIV)

Recently, the sermon series at church was called *No Small Acts*. Each week focused on a lesser-known character in the book of Acts who God called to do his work in the world. Our pastor encouraged the congregation to develop a habit of seeking to know God's will, of listening to God's calling.

On one of these Sundays, we sang the hymn, *Here I Am, Lord*. It stirred my heart, and I decided to learn to play the song on my harp. I practiced it over and over, memorizing the finger placement and developed chords to accompany the melody. The words say, "Whom shall I send? Here I am, Lord... Is it I, Lord... I will go, Lord... if you lead me."[1]

A few days later, the chaplain at the senior facility where my mom lives asked if I would lead the Sunday church service while he was gone. Panic flooded my heart and my mind raced to make a list of all the reasons I couldn't say, "Yes."

This was a request way beyond my abilities. I wasn't qualified. I have performance anxiety and fear of public speaking. Others are better suited.

Despite my certainty that I would say, "No," I prayed, asking God to make it clear whether I should lead.

As I prayed, I remembered the sermon series from church and squirmed. Later that day, I sat down and played the hymn. "Is it I, Lord…I will go, Lord…if you lead me."

I considered the elderly living at the senior facility who could no longer drive and wanted to worship on Sundays. Feeling convicted, I wondered if I could trust God to help me. Uncomfortable, uncertain, and resistant, I knew God's will in this request from the chaplain. I said, "Yes," and started preparing for the service.

As I prepared, I read the lectionary for the Sunday I would be speaking. The Old Testament lesson was from Exodus 3:1-15. Moses was out tending sheep, minding his own business, living his structured life, when he spotted a burning bush.

God called out to him.

Moses responded, "Here I am."

God asked Moses to go to Pharaoh.

Moses responded, "Who am I that I should go?" Good point, Moses!

God said, "I will be with you." How interesting that the lectionary for this week addressed my fears, my listening, and my story with God.

Looking back, I see how God used the sermon series to set the stage for my choice about serving. The hymn's words and music echoed over and over in my heart. The request came to serve God and care for his people. The response of *no* screamed loudly from within, but I whispered, "Yes."

God's confirmation of my whispered response came as I read the lectionary and heard him speak with thundering assurance, "I will be with you." His presence is always enough, his grace is sufficient for me, and his power is made perfect in my weakness.

PRAYER

Thank you, God, for your Word filled with stories of you working in people's minds and hearts. Thank you for your promised presence for me as I say yes to your work. Help me always listen for and recognize your voice and have the courage to say *yes* when you call. In Jesus' name, Amen.

UNLEASH YOUR PEN

Write about a time when you sensed God's call to you. What work does God have for you to do?

Looking To Jesus

> Looking to Jesus, the founder and perfecter of our faith, who for the joy that was set before him endured the cross, despising the shame, and is seated at the right hand of the throne of God.
>
> — HEBREWS 12:2 (ESV)

When I look to Jesus, who do I see? Where do I look? Prosopagnosia is a condition where a person struggles to recognize the faces of others and to understand facial expressions. It's a neurological disorder but also could apply spiritually when one struggles to see and recognize Jesus. It takes time and effort to gaze on Jesus, consider who he is, and develop an intimate relationship with him.

A hymn written in 1922, "Turn Your Eyes Upon Jesus," states in the refrain: "Turn your eyes upon Jesus, look full in his wonderful face, and the things of earth will grow strangely dim, in the light of his glory and grace."[1] The phrase, "Look full in his wonderful face," catches my attention because when I turn my eyes upon Jesus, I don't usually look fully into his face. When I look at Jesus, I tend to see a male of middle eastern descent with a beard. At times, I visualize him on the cross with his head bowed low in suffering, or I see his back as he walks ahead of me. I might see Jesus in the emerging light of dawn as Mary did after the resurrection when she didn't recognize him. My vision is dim, blurred, looking but not clearly seeing, and my eyes tend to roam about.

I feel like I am missing something, for when I gaze into the faces of those I love and see them looking back at me with mirrored love, I feel blessed. Intimacy is transferred as eyes glance and then maintain a direct gaze. Imagine the recognition and transfer of love that occurs when someone holds a baby, stares into this small face, and catches bright and curious eyes looking back. All eyes widen in shared recognition of the other, love flowing out, and flowing in beyond explanation.

Now imagine the many people we pass by in life on the streets and even in our own homes where we don't take the time or make the effort to look into their faces and see them for who they are in the moment. Without awareness and intention, the opportunity for an intimate moment of knowing and being known is missed. These moments of connection are lost forever, and life can become increasingly lonely.

It is easy for roaming eyes to wander to the distractions of the world, especially with the myriad bright screens that demand fixed gazes and gobble up our time and energy. As I consider Jesus, I am challenged to look fully into his wonderful face, to fix my gaze on him. This practice reveals Jesus' face of love, joy, peace, healing, invitation, sadness, suffering, or prayer.

His face is glowing, transfigured, and divine. His eyes gaze back, full of grace. No one looks at me like this. Jesus knows me as no one else does, and his gaze extends beyond time, knowing me before I was born and welcoming me into eternity.

He knows me better than I know myself. He sees all that is hidden deep in my heart and all the secrets I hold close in fear and shame. When I offer these secrets to him, he offers forgiveness back to me. His face is full of love and blessed assurance.

PRAYER

Loving Jesus, you are the source and the goal of my faith. I seek your face today as I turn toward you. Thank you for always being present to me. May your glory and grace capture my gaze and hold me in your love. In your name, I pray, Amen.

UNLEASH YOUR PEN

What do you see and feel when you fix your eyes upon Jesus? What helps you hold your gaze on his face?

Belonging to God's Family

> The Spirit you received brought about your adoption to sonship. And by him we cry, "Abba, Father." The Spirit himself testifies with our spirit that we are God's children. Now, if we are God's children, then we are heirs—heirs of God and co-heirs with Christ.
>
> — ROMANS 8:15B-17A (NIV)

Loneliness is said to be an epidemic, and people feel increasingly detached from family and friends. I have felt overwhelmed with loneliness at times in my life, wondering where I belong and to whom I belong. God's Word helps us with these feelings, offering us adoption into his family. We can belong as a child of the Father, a sibling and co-heirs with Christ when we choose to accept Jesus as Lord and Savior of our life. When we take this faith step, God promises to be available in all circumstances.

Certain rights and privileges come with being part of a family, both in this world and in God's kingdom. Legacy includes things that are inherited, passed on, or handed down from our family or the past. We can receive a legacy of money, sentimental objects, religious beliefs, physical characteristics, or many other things from family. Adam and Eve passed on a legacy of sin to every generation.

When we choose to believe in Jesus, our sins are forgiven, and our hearts are transformed and made righteous before God. We belong to God, being adopted into God's family. As heirs of God and co-heirs with Christ, we immediately receive Christ's legacy of righteousness and a rich spiritual inheritance from God, our Father. As adoptive children, this includes the kingdom of heaven, a place to live now and for eternity.

God's legacy includes his will and intentions for our life. God's will is written in his Word, a treasure trove of stories, values, prophesy, commands, and promises.

God's adoptive children receive his Holy Spirit. Jesus says in John 14:26-27, "But, the Advocate, the Holy Spirit, whom the Father will send in my name, will teach you all things and will remind you of everything I have said to you. Peace I leave with you; my peace I give to you."

Believers inherit the Holy Spirit as an advocate who teaches and guides our hearts. The word *remember* is used many times in the Bible and is a consistent, persistent command from the Lord. He wants his children to read, know, and bring to mind his Word. God wants us to know who he is and to recall his work in past generations and our lives. These memories strengthen our faith and hope. Jesus also gives us his peace, allowing us to connect to the Father as we live in this world.

Our legacy from the Holy Spirit is described further in Galatians 5:22 (MSG), "What happens when we live God's way? He brings gifts into our lives, much the same way that fruit appears in an orchard—things like affection for others, exuberance about life, serenity. We develop a willingness to stick with things, a sense of compassion in the heart, and a conviction that a basic holiness permeates things and people. We find ourselves involved in loyal commitments."

The Spirit transforms us to be more like Jesus. God's children receive the legacy and inheritance of Christ Jesus. All these gifts, this enormous inheritance, are available for every child of God right now. Will you receive it?

PRAYER

Abba Father, Jesus, Spirit, my heart fills with gratitude at the rich legacy you have offered to all believers. Enable me to receive this inheritance today and every day. I love you and am forever yours. Amen.

UNLEASH YOUR PEN

Have you experienced feelings of loneliness and not belonging? God wants you, as his child, to belong forever to his family. Write about what this means to you.

Beauty in God's Sight

> Our beauty should not come from outward adornment, such as elaborate hairstyles and the wearing of gold jewelry or fine clothes. Rather, it should be that of your inner self, the unfading beauty of a gentle and quiet spirit, which is of great worth in God's sight.
>
> — 1 PETER 3:3-4 (NIV)

This season of my life is one of pause. I wait, curious about what might come next. I stand on the threshold between building and letting go. I have retired and am discerning what I want to hold onto and what to cultivate and what things are better left behind. Aging involves loss. Energy, beauty, and strength fade. Even relationships fade as people die, leaving only precious memories. During this time of waiting, the verse above captured my attention, speaking of the unfading beauty of a gentle and quiet spirit.

How do I define beauty? How does our culture? The Merriam-Webster Dictionary defines beauty as *the quality or group of qualities in a person or thing that gives pleasure to the senses or the mind.*[1] This seems to include inward and outward beauty.

There are many ways we try to create outward beauty so we can feel pleasure when looking in the mirror. There are creams, cosmetics, and shampoos to enhance beauty, along with more extreme cosmetic surgery treatments. Retail stores and online businesses display current fashion trends. There are nails to be painted, hair to be colored, tattoos to be inked, and eyelashes to be extended. The list goes on. These can drain our money and time and become traps that entice and capture us. Yet, we all desire beauty in ourselves and in our lives. It is for each of us to decide where to draw the line between healthy self-care and pursuing beauty at greater costs.

God's Word says in 1 Peter that our beauty shouldn't come from outward adornment but rather should come from our inner self. It says the beauty of a gentle and quiet spirit is unfading. This implies it is eternal. Although it won't cost anything financially, achieving this beauty will demand sacrifice. It doesn't need to be renewed or applied day by day. Still, it necessitates cultivation; gentleness and a quiet spirit don't arise spontaneously.

This internal beauty is of great worth in God's sight and is the beauty that God sees. The Lord does not see as we see. We look on the outward appearance, but the Lord looks at the heart (I Samuel 16:7). In this season of discerning how to move forward in my life, I want to cultivate gentleness and quietness of spirit. I pray for the Holy Spirit to help redefine my thoughts about beauty to align with God's thoughts. Gentleness is a fruit of the Spirit and increases in us as we allow the Spirit access to our hearts, minds, and souls.

Inner beauty, unfading light
Her quiet, gentle spirit glows gratitude
Content with all God has given
It is enough, she is enough
Freedom from anxiety
Freedom from striving
Freedom from competing
God sees within, God knows
His smile showers down sparkly love
Into her heart

PRAYER

Loving Father, I desire a gentle and quiet spirit. Help me to grow in grace and beauty that is inward and pleasing to you. In Jesus' name, Amen.

UNLEASH YOUR PEN

Write about the unfading beauty of a gentle and quiet spirit. Consider writing a poem.

Always Thankful

> Give thanks in all circumstances; for this is God's
> will for you in Christ Jesus.
>
> — 1 THESSALONIANS 5:18 (NIV)

Thanksgiving is my favorite holiday. It's a holiday where family and friends gather without the stress of needing to write cards, put up decorations, or buy gifts. I love cooking and hosting this time of feasting. As I prepare, the concept of thankfulness is always on my mind.

In 1 Thessalonians 5:18, God says to *give thanks always, in all circumstances.* There is no gray area, no wiggle room in this command where *always* and *in all circumstances* are clearly spoken. It is a command for each day, not just for Thanksgiving. This verse sparks a wrestling match in my heart, as each year brings challenging circumstances where I do not feel thankful. I have experienced great losses with people I love dearly, sharing tears during times of suffering. Giving thanks doesn't seem a reasonable response to circumstances involving pain, suffering, and death.

Prayerfully, I consider this verse. It doesn't say to be thankful *for* all circumstances, it says to be thankful *in* all circumstances. The word *in* is the key word. It is easy to feel thankful in times of peace, joy, and when prayer has been answered. Thankfulness in all circumstances reflects the state of a heart in relationship with God. It is about golden treasures carried within.

Despite hard circumstances, I can be thankful for God's Word and his gift of faith. I can be thankful that God is sovereign now and forever. He who is abundant in grace, mercy, and lovingkindness is in control. God knows all, sees all, and cares about every detail of my life. He promises to be present with me all the time, in hard and joyful circumstances. I am never alone. I am offered forgiveness, salvation, and restored peace with God. During hard times of lament and wrestling with God, I am overwhelmed by his love and the resources he offers. When I connect with God, his divine light offers hope beyond the dark fog of circumstances. Hope illuminated and expressions of my love and trust become a poem, a prayer, or a song of thanksgiving to God. Giving thanks is God's will for me and all believers in Christ Jesus.

Meditating on God's presence and perspective on life births a feeling of gratitude in my heart. Gratitude is like a warm cup of tea on a bitterly cold winter day, appealing to all of the senses. Imagine with me. Hold the warm cup in your hands, breathe in the humid air and lemon scent. Anticipate the taste and feel in your mouth. Sense the warmth travel downward and all around as it warms your insides. Gratitude warms the body, heart, soul, and spirit. It infuses a sense of peace—God's peace, which is beyond understanding. Thank you, God, for your peace.

PRAYER

I praise you, Lord. I give thanks to you, Lord. You are good, loving, gracious, and merciful. Your love endures forever and lives in me, warming my heart and imparting strength and courage to encounter every circumstance. Help me to grow in my capacity to practice gratitude and to see and feel your presence in my life and in the world. In Jesus' name, Amen.

UNLEASH YOUR PEN

Consider and write about a specific situation where it felt hard to give God thanks. What does it feel like to give God thanks in your life today?

Help From the Lord

> I lift up my eyes to the mountains—where does my help come from? My help comes from the LORD, the Maker of heaven and earth. The LORD will watch over your coming and going both now and forevermore.
>
> — PSALM 121:1-2, 8 (NIV)

Help is a word that can be considered a command, an invitation, a question, or a plea. I have prayed it often as a plea and often have felt "unhelped." I prayed for the power of God to overcome my weakness, and I haven't noticed his power in the midst of my weakness. I prayed for strength and haven't felt strong. I trust God is answering these prayers in some way, but I haven't seen an answer. So, I wait, continuing to pray and to raise my eyes to the hills where my help comes from.

Not long ago, I was at a physical therapy appointment and tears filled my eyes, surprising me. I am a stoic who holds my feelings in and processes them in private. The physical therapist was kind, and seemed to care, trying so hard to help me. I felt blessed. Then it came to my mind that three other times in the past five days people went out of their way to help me. They went above and beyond what I expected and considered appropriate for the setting. For some reason, I thought people would respond to my problems with a *bare minimum* offering, but each person exceeded my idea of expected care. They took the time to encourage me and offered me tools which gave me hope.

Aha! For some reason, it clicked in my blind mind that God answered my prayer for help. I wasn't going to get a lightning bolt of power flashing down from heaven into my body or a sudden infusion of superpower strength, but I was being helped. Help came through these people God brought into my life. They provided comfort, compassion, a sense of God's presence, and practical advice.

I worked as a healthcare provider for several years. People sought me for help, but I rarely sought the help of others. Now, being older and with new areas of physical struggle, my fierce independence leaves me lacking. It leaves me humbled. Today, I lift my eyes to the hills, and I know where my help comes from. It comes from the Lord, the maker of heaven and earth. God brought people into my life who help me. Thank you, God. Thank you for these people.

PRAYER

Lord, thank you for opening my eyes so I might see you at work in my life. Thank you for your provision of people who help and care. Thank you for watching over my coming and going now and forever. In Jesus' name, Amen.

UNLEASH YOUR PEN

Where do you need help? Raise your eyes to the hills, open your eyes, and look around. Where might you be receiving help from the Lord?

Dawn Rogers

Dawn Rogers has been journaling as a spiritual practice for more than 20 years. Her pen serves as a conduit for pouring out thoughts, feelings, and questions to God. Through journaling, scripture, prayers, and raw reflections, she has experienced profound spiritual connection and growth. After 19 years in global logistics and nine years with Wells Fargo, Dawn left the corporate world in 2014 to pursue a more purpose-filled life. She lives in Minneapolis, Minnesota with her husband Mark.

In 2016, Dawn tragically lost her 15-year-old daughter, Olivia, to suicide. Despite this heartbreaking loss, Dawn has found strength and hope through her faith. Isaiah 40:31 (NIV),

"Those who hope in the LORD will renew their strength," brought Dawn out of the depths of despair shortly after Olivia went home to Jesus.

A mother to three other adult children and a proud grandmother, Dawn enjoys cooking nourishing meals, reading, adventuring, gardening, golfing, and taking walks in nature. She treasures time spent with family, friends, and her playful dog. For more than 23 years, Dawn has served as a vocalist at her church, combining her love for prayer and for worship to draw closer to God and encourage others in their faith.

As an emcee, speaker, and writer, Dawn's messages radiate hope and resilience. She lives by the mantra "LIVe – Live In Victory every day" and inspires others to embrace this way of living, no matter their circumstances. Committed to holistic well-being—mental, physical, emotional, spiritual, relational, social, and financial—Dawn believes everyone has inherent value and purpose. No matter your choices, experiences, or hardships, you matter. Her purpose is to help others take the next step toward finding victory, joy, hope, and peace every day.

Visit her website at dawnmrogers.com.

Abundant Life in Crisis

> The thief comes only to steal and kill and destroy. I came that they may have life and have it abundantly.

— JOHN 10:10 (ESV)

The first part of this scripture starts with some strong, bleak words, and then comes the truth and promise from Jesus. It is a great reminder to keep reading. If we stop and only read the first sentence, we can be left feeling afraid, deflated, and hopeless. These words of truth are spoken directly from Jesus. First, he shares the truth of the plans and purposes of the enemy, who is real and active. Then Jesus shares the truth of his plan and purposes. This powerful truth from Jesus is an example of the truth spoken in love. Truth can hurt, triggering fear and hopelessness if we stop listening. We need to read and listen for the truth, the complete truth. We need to hold tight to the truth and be ready at any time to share it with others, especially in a time of crisis or trouble.

It was a lovely late summer afternoon. My husband, Mark, was out of town for work. I was home alone for the weekend. It had been two months since the tragic loss of my precious daughter. Olivia was 15 years old at the time of her death. I found myself going outside to pass time and breathe in the fresh air. As I watered the front lawn, the realization that Olivia was gone hit me hard, she wasn't coming home. I doubled over with deep, agonizing grief. This reality brought an instant longing that collided with the pain of grief and loss. It was an unbearable, raw pain that made me feel like I could literally crawl out of my skin. I felt deep, sharp pains from the jagged shards of my shattered heart.

At this moment, my heart empathized with how Jesus felt the night he was betrayed and experienced that separation from his Father. I felt all of it. I panicked. My mind reeled with what-ifs, regret, doubt, and condemnation. A tsunami of emotions competed to take over any sense of rationality or peace. My mind became inundated with flashbacks. I was in an all-out battle. The enemy was out to destroy me, and I couldn't find my way back. I was in a crisis.

Subtly, the Holy Spirit's whisper reached me. I knew this was not a time to be alone. I needed help. I needed someone to be with me. As I glanced up, I saw the van of our worship leader, Eric, parked at my church across the street. He and his wife, Kris, are dear friends of mine. I called Eric's mobile phone, and thankfully, he answered. Through my continual sobs, I was able to communicate that I needed help. He was at my side within minutes. Shortly after, Kris arrived. They sat with me and held my hand, listening, praying, holding me. They caught my tears and kept the tissues flowing to wipe my nose.

My dear friends reminded me of the priceless, unique relationship I had with Olivia. They described the deep love and special connection we had as mother and daughter. Kris recalled explicit memories of Olivia. Each took turns sharing scripture, assuring me of Jesus' love and the hope of his promises, including eternal life for each of us. They painted a beautiful picture of Olivia, safe in his arms now and forever. The truth won out. My tears stopped. Kris brought me a glass of water, and reminded me to take deep cleansing breaths, which led me to a healthy breathing rhythm. We shared a late dinner that had been provided by a church member as part of a meal train.

Abundant life showed up in a multitude of simple ways that day: authentic, selfless friends, comforting arms, deep breaths, cleansing tears, a cold glass of water, provision of nourishment, soft tissues, sunshine turning to dusk, and truth—powerful promises from Jesus. Friendship can be the thread the Lord uses to show himself real and personal in someone's life to rescue them. Kris and Eric were the hands, feet, and heart of Jesus to me. He physically reached me through them right there in my living room. The enemy was out to destroy me, but Jesus rescued me and provided abundant life. The truth of abundant life is that it can be in the simplest, most basic provisions.

PRAYER

Dear Jesus, thank you for your truth and provision. I know the enemy is out to kill, steal and destroy, yet you are my Rescuer and came to give me life in abundance in every situation. May you continue to show me the way and light. In Jesus' name, Amen.

UNLEASH YOUR PEN

Pause and reflect on a difficult experience you have had and ask Jesus to show you abundant life in the midst of it. Let your pen flow in reflection and gratitude.

Ask Listen Look

> The LORD your God is among you, a warrior who saves. He will rejoice over you with gladness. He will be quiet in his love. He will delight in you with singing.

— ZEPHANIAH 3:17 (CSB)

It was early morning and time to let Koda, my sweet yellow lab, out for his morning business. I was just out of bed, moving slow, and felt groggy. Before I opened the door, I heard it. Her familiar song was strong, clear and close. Her dainty voice delivered a perfect melody. I opened the door, and Koda slowly walks down the icy steps onto the patio. I stepped forward and stood in the doorway with the brisk, late-winter Minnesota morning air tickling my face.

With my glasses still on the nightstand, everything was a blur. God attuned my ears to her voice. I raised my head and glanced up toward the sound. There she was. I saw the silhouette of her body and the crest of her head against the remnants of the night's darkness. Even through the blurriness I could see it was a beautiful female cardinal singing a song over me, *just for me.* Her song was sweet, intentional, and majestic. This beautiful morning blessing caused me to pause and take notice. The grandeur of this intimate gift was surfacing.

I often see cardinals in my backyard. Most often, they are the vibrant red males who perch themselves off in the distance in a tree or on my back fence. On this particular day, this precious *female* was close, very close. The moment was intimate. She perched herself on a cable wire only a few feet above my patio to greet me with a beautiful morning song through her varied trills. As I reveled in her song, I recalled the words I had written in my journal twenty-four hours earlier.

I vented and poured my heart out to the Lord with overwhelming thoughts and questions. My pen was a conduit to my heart and mind, allowing my raw feelings to pour out with the force of a fire hydrant through the trickle of a leaky garden hose onto the page. The ink flowing aided me in processing my emotions. God quieted me in his love. My heart grew lighter, and my writing turned to gratitude. I thanked him for the early signs of spring. My pen crafted a specific, simple prayer.

> *Lord, please bring the cardinals. They bring me such peace and joy. I pray they will come to visit me. I love their unique song and bright color. They remind me of heaven, letting me know someone I love is near and watching me. May they show themselves to me and stay nearby. They always catch my attention and put a smile on my face. I hope I see one soon!*

126

I asked, he heard, and he answered! God gave me what I asked for in a precious female cardinal presented so uniquely to me. I was immediately overwhelmed by the Lord's presence and his personal gift. What a glorious way to start the day! God caught my attention, attuned my ears to hear, and focused my eyes to see his blessing. He delighted in me singing through the cardinal.

PRAYER

Heavenly Father, thank you for hearing my prayers and knowing my heart. I'm overwhelmed with your personal gifts and blessings. I'm grateful for the creative ways you show up to speak to me and for your gentleness in getting my attention. You are good and faithful all the time! May I ask, listen, and look with great expectation. In Jesus' name, Amen.

UNLEASH YOUR PEN

What brings you peace and puts a smile on your face? Write a specific prayer asking him for something personal that will bring you joy. Ask. Listen. Look. He delights in blessing you! Come back a few days later and reflect on your prayer.

The Ultimate Gift

 A person's gift opens doors for him and brings him before the great.

— PROVERBS 18:16 (CSB)

You are invited into a private conversation between me and the Lord. It's my journey to discovering heaven's perspective as I read Proverbs 18:16. I hope it inspires you to have many of your own conversations with God. He loves you and has much to reveal to you.

As I read the verse I thought, "Oooh, how exciting! My gift will open doors for me and bring me before the great! What gift? What doors? What great? Who? Finally, I will have a purpose and will be rewarded for it! I need to process this verse through my pen."

My mind reeled with questions and wonder. My heart was

hopeful and tingly. I jotted a simple, common prayer while the Holy Spirit stirred within me.

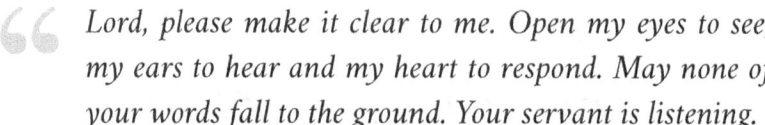

> *Lord, please make it clear to me. Open my eyes to see, my ears to hear and my heart to respond. May none of your words fall to the ground. Your servant is listening.*

I thought, "I have gifts. We all have gifts. Proverbs 18:16 speaks about a singular gift. Hmmmm, which gift? Oh, maybe each individual gift will open a different door and bring me before different greats. But it says *"the* great," again singular— one. Each gift I have will open different doors and will bring me before the same great? Oh boy, this is confusing. This short verse is having a profound impact on me. What is he trying to tell me? I need clarity."

I continue with more writing and prayer. I ponder as I find a rhythm with my rocker on my patio. I sit back, close my eyes, and tilt my head to allow the morning air to brush against my face while I invite the Holy Spirit to speak in and around me.

My mind continued to reel with thoughts and questions. "I'm trying to be still, Lord, please calm my thoughts and bring me to the truth you want me to glean from this verse in this moment."

Initially, I found myself processing this verse through the world's views and teachings. I was thinking of worldly gifts and worldly greats. I pondered, "Where are the personality tests and spiritual gifts assessments I completed? What words have I received from friends and family offering to encourage me and affirm my gifts? Let's see: prayer, mercy, authenticity and transparency, God's spokesperson, my light and energy, faith."

I prayed, "I need time alone with you, God, time away. Allure me away. Speak tenderly to me."

I felt a longing to be away from home to spend uninterrupted time with God to page through old journals, notes, assessments, and cards from others to identify my gifts. Again, I sat in stillness and took in a few breaths. Engaging with God's presence, he redirected my focus to read John 14. I was invited into a conversation between Jesus and his disciples when he offered comfort and assurance as he prepared them for his departure. Jesus promised that the Father would send another counselor, the Holy Spirit, to be with them forever. There was a flutter in my spirit. This was an epiphany that shifted my perspective from my worldly views of gifts and greats into the heavenly realm of gifts and *the* greatness of God.

I exclaimed, "Eureka! This is the *gift* the Father wanted me to see, the ultimate gift. The Holy Spirit is the *gift* that will open doors for me and bring me before the great. I just need to be still, listen, receive, and obey. The Holy Spirit guides me. I need only to follow, and I am brought before the great."

On this day I started seeing the word *gift* in a fresh way. There are a variety of gifts he offers me. I am excited at what he will do in and through me as I open my hands and heart to receive, embrace and live in his gift of the Holy Spirit.

PRAYER

Dear Jesus, thank you for going before the Father on my behalf to ask him to send another advocate, the gift, who will open doors for me and bring me before the great. Please clear my mind of the world's gifts and open my eyes to see afresh all the beautiful, divine gifts from heaven. May I be ready to receive, embrace, and enjoy them. In your precious name, Amen.

UNLEASH YOUR PEN

Read and ponder Proverbs 18:16. Be still and meditate on it. Let the Holy Spirit counsel you and guide your pen. Discover the personal message he has for your heart.

The Ministry of Presence

 They went to a place called Gethsemane, and Jesus said to his disciples, "Sit here while I pray." He took Peter, James and John along with him, and he began to be deeply distressed and troubled.

— MARK 14:32-33 (NIV)

The very night Jesus would be arrested, rejected, and crucified, he went to Gethsemane to pray. Jesus knew Judas had betrayed him and would soon be arriving with a crowd of men who would arrest him and bring him before the Sanhedrin. His disciples were with him. Jesus told them to sit while he prayed. As he went on to a place a little further, he invited a trusted trio, Peter, James, and John, to come with him. As the Son of Man, he was deeply distressed and troubled and chose not to be alone in this moment. As the Son of God, he knew the Father's will and that he would be obedient, yet in his anguish, Jesus cried out to ask his abba, Father, to take this cup from him.

Gethsemane was a physical, public place. But Jesus invited his close friends into a profoundly personal space—a place of raw, anguished prayer. It would be uncomfortable to witness, and Jesus knew the trio couldn't fully grasp the weight of what was to come, but still, he asked them to be near. Perhaps he longed for the comfort of their presence, a shared moment of humanity, even as he faced his divine mission.

The Lord brought this scripture to mind and brought a new understanding of it to me one morning as I lay in bed, overcome with grief. It was a few weeks before Easter, ten months after my precious Olivia went to heaven and met Jesus face to face. At only 15 years old, my daughter died by her own hand. The weight of that separation—body, soul, and spirit—was unbearable. Tears streamed down my face, and I couldn't summon the strength to get up.

It was in the quiet of that moment when the Lord brought Mark 14:32-33 to mind. As I pictured Jesus inviting his disciples into *his* sorrow.

God whispered to my heart, "Let others be present with you in your grief, as I did."

I reflected back on the multitude of family and friends who had come to be with me over those ten months. Some didn't know what to say but would sit near me or hold me. Others snuggled in and wept alongside me. No one could take the pain or longing for my daughter away, but their presence brought comfort, a reminder that I wasn't alone in my garden of sorrow.

In time, God also revealed something else. Just as Jesus' disciples witnessed his anguish, the people who came alongside me were learning something profound. My pain gave them the opportunity to practice the ministry of presence—to mourn with those who mourn, to love without fixing, and to simply be there.

This is the ministry of presence: being willing to sit with someone in their pain, even when there's nothing you can say or do to change it. Sometimes, it means letting others into your sorrow and allowing them to express love like Jesus.

PRAYER

Lord, thank you for the example of Jesus in the Garden of Gethsemane. Help me to invite others into my pain, even when it feels vulnerable. Teach me to sit with others in their grief and exercise the ministry of presence. Thank you for the comfort of your presence and the reminder that we are never alone. In Jesus' name, Amen.

UNLEASH YOUR PEN

Think of a time when you've been comforted by someone's presence. What did they do, or not do, that made it meaningful? Now, think of someone in your life who may be grieving or hurting. How can you offer that someone the ministry of presence this week? Write a prayer asking God to guide you in this sacred act of love.

Walking with Jesus

> Do not fear, for I am with you; do not be dismayed, for I am your God. I will strengthen you and help you; I will uphold you with my righteous right hand.
>
> — ISAIAH 41:10 (NIV)

This devotional is a personal psalm of gratitude and transformation that reflects my journey of walking with Jesus. Writing in this poetic form allows me to express my faith in a different, creative way.

I walk with Jesus, as I move and as I stand,
He strengthens me with his unshakeable, steady hand.
I've been given so much; I'm blessed beyond measure,
Jesus, my one true love, is my greatest treasure.
I'm forever grateful Jesus paid the price for my sin,

and lifted me up from the pit I was in.
What I treasure most can't be held in my hands or seen,
Seeing me live my best life in Jesus' eyes is what I hope
others perceive.
They will know my life of luxury is in his gifts of
strength and grace,
I share my wealth of joy as it shines from my heart to
my face.
They will see me being a faithful steward of all heaven
has for me,
As I abide in the Father, snuggling in his arms or
kneeling on bended knee.
My spirit anchored, unyielding, and free,
I've been transformed by the strength he has given me.
Amidst the blessings, doubts still arise,
Satan is cunning, and whispers lies.
My mind wanders, and I compare myself to others,
God is faithful and reminds me how I'm uniquely
created with gifts to love and serve with my sisters
and brothers.
Forgiveness I offer when others do harm,
Enduring, sacrificial love from God is the source of my
charm.
Walking with Jesus has transformed my way,
His presence is my strength, my guide every day.
In every struggle, his love sets me free,
Walking with Jesus—my game-changing strategy.

PRAYER

Lord, thank you for your strength, forgiveness, and the unique gifts only you give. Help me to live in your love and share it with others, even on my hardest days. In Jesus' precious name, Amen.

UNLEASH YOUR PEN

Write a personal psalm about how walking with Jesus is a game changer for you. Include moments of struggle, joy, and his presence through it all.

Arise and Shine

 Arise, shine, for your light has come, and the glory of the Lord shines over you.

— ISAIAH 60:1 (CSB)

Having lived in Minnesota my whole life, I've grown to love the rhythm of our four seasons. Each one brings its own beauty, weather patterns, flowers, critters, lakes, skylines, and unique activities. While the calendar marks the changing seasons, many let it dictate their mood, attire or plans. For example, there's the adage: "No white pants or open-toed sandals before Memorial Day or after Labor Day." Who came up with this standard? Personally, I don't follow such rules. If it's warm and sunny, I'm wearing sandals. And if my white pants match my bright blouse in March, I'm wearing them too!

It's not rebellion; it's simply the unique me God designed. Psalm 139:13 reminds me that God created my innermost being, knitting me together with care and attention. His creation gives me pleasure, helps me grow and mature and reveals more of who he is. As I've embraced this truth, I've come to know myself more deeply—the me he sees and loves. My light shines in how I communicate, create, and live out my faith. My uniqueness is displayed in my attire, cooking, house décor, and activities.

For years, I let life's circumstances—weather, trends, others' opinions—dictate my thoughts, how I feel, what I wear, and how I act. I became a chameleon, constantly adapting to fit in. But as I've grown in faith, I've learned to arise and shine, letting God's light guide me. His glory breaks through like springtime after a long winter. Whether it's snowing or sunny, there is springtime in my soul.

Whether I am reading his Word, walking in nature, or fellowshipping with others, my soul is refreshed. Living authentically as the unique person he created spurs me on to arise, shine, and move forward with hope and purpose.

PRAYER

Father God, thank you for uniquely creating me in your image. I'm grateful for all your creation and how you speak tenderly to my heart. You are gentle and kind. I am seeking your ways and will for my life. What is the best use of my time, gifts, and energy today? May I live fully in who you created me to be and bring glory to you in all I do. Amen.

UNLEASH YOUR PEN

What puts a spring in your step or refreshes your soul? Do you need a fresh dose of truth or time alone in nature? Spend some time asking the Lord what he wants you to know right now. Listen. Let him speak to you as you unleash your pen. It is true. His glory shines over you. Your light has come. Arise and shine!

Prepare the Way

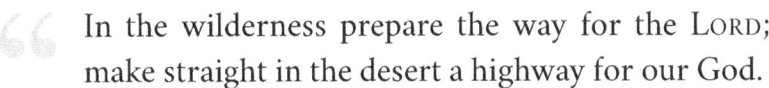

> In the wilderness prepare the way for the LORD;
> make straight in the desert a highway for our God.
>
> — ISAIAH 40:3 (NIV)

For weeks, I felt stuck—like I had been wandering in a wilderness with my new business. Projects waiting, decisions unmade, and momentum stalled—all had caused me to feel irresponsible. I had been frustrated with myself, questioning my rhythm and commitment. I felt behind and reluctant. Yet, in my devotional time, Isaiah 40:3 caught my attention and shifted my perspective. In this passage, Isaiah speaks tenderly to God's people, exiled in Babylon and longing for deliverance. His words were a comfort and a promise that God would provide a way out of their captivity. He wasn't just calling them to prepare their physical path; he was calling them to prepare their hearts to *see* God's mighty work.

This made me reflect on my own wilderness season. It felt like a place of aimlessness. But through prayer, I began to see it differently. What if the wilderness is not about being lost or stalled but about becoming prepared? After all, the wilderness is where some of God's most extraordinary work happens. Elijah heard God's still, small voice in the wilderness. Moses met him in a burning bush. Even Jesus, before launching his ministry, spent 40 days in the desert. What if my waiting and wondering have been opportunities to remove obstacles so I can see God more clearly?

Using my pen as a conduit to process my thoughts and prayers with scripture, I realized that my *wandering* was actually a season of rest, refreshment and stewardship—taking care of my body, mind, and relationships after an intense period of activity. This wasn't wasted time; it was holy preparation. It was a time to declutter my heart and life, making room to *see* God's work. God is always at work.

I found myself asking him, "Which obstacles in my heart or life are keeping me from seeing your work?"

Isaiah's call to prepare the way for the Lord reminded me of the intentionality it takes to host loved ones during the holidays. Preparation includes detailed lists, gifts to purchase, a menu of delicious foods, decorating the house, and making space for connection, fellowship, and joy. Similarly, preparing a highway for God means clearing distractions, softening my heart, and being present so I can experience his work in my life. As I thought about how to prepare for God's work, I found myself repenting of obstacles keeping me from seeing his mighty work and keeping me from moving forward.

Another layer of this scripture came alive for me through

the Hebrew word qâvâh (kaw-vaw'), which means to wait, hope, or expect.[1]

It's used in Isaiah 40:31 (NIV): "Those who hope (qâvâh) in the LORD will renew their strength."

Waiting for God isn't passive; it's active trust. It's like pulling a cord tight, building anticipation until it's released. I realized my waiting in the wilderness wasn't wasted—it was filled with wonder and expectancy. God's character and faithfulness are my anchors, not my own striving.

As I continue this journey, I see the wilderness not as a place of reluctance, doubt or guilt, but as an opportunity to prepare. To clear away distractions, I focus on his Word and trust that he's working behind the scenes—even in the quiet, dry places. God does some of his greatest work in the wilderness, and I don't want to miss a single moment of it.

PRAYER

Lord, thank you for meeting me in the wilderness. Help me to see this season as preparation, not punishment. Show me what needs to be cleared away so I can experience your work in my life. Teach me to wait with hope and trust in your faithfulness. Use this time to draw me closer to you. Amen.

UNLEASH YOUR PEN

Write about a time when you felt like you were wandering in a wilderness season. How did you see God show up? What can you do now to prepare the way for him to work?

It Won't Be Long

> Jesus went on to say, "In a little while you will see me no more, and then after a little while you will see me."
>
> — JOHN 16:16 (NIV)

Six weeks after my 15-year-old daughter Olivia died, I returned to the church stage to sing with the worship team on a Sunday morning. After the worship set, I found my way to a seat with my husband to sit down for the sermon. I was exhausted and weepy. Worship felt different. The words were still real and true. My heart was so tender. I clung to my faith and the faithfulness of his words and offered my worship as a living sacrifice.

As I sat down, I saw my friend, Bev, for the first time since the traumatic, sudden loss of my beautiful Olivia. I looked at Bev, our eyes locked. Bev is a wise, elderly woman I adore and respect. She reached out her arms to me, took my hands in hers, and held them tight. She pulled me very close and told me how sorry she was. Looking deep into my eyes while shaking her head, Bev went on to say she didn't understand, didn't have any answers, and didn't know what to say.

She continued to share that as she had been praying for me and my family, the Lord kept telling her, "It won't be long. It won't be long!" She was certain. She was bold. She was genuine and believable as she repeated it over and over.

I found solace in the honesty of this deeply faithful, and godly woman, who admitted, "I don't understand, and I don't know what to say." I was so thankful to Bev for not trying to figure it out or have all the answers. There weren't any. It would remain a mystery as to why the Lord allowed Olivia to die that tragic night a few weeks earlier.

It won't be long... my mind raced, and I wasn't sure what this meant, but I clung to it. It won't be long before I join Olivia? It won't be long before Jesus comes back? This was already a fervent prayer of mine that Jesus would come back soon. Admittedly, I just wanted to be done with life on earth and join him face to face with my precious daughter by his side. I hurt so badly. The broken shards of my heart cut through me every day, and it was a huge feat to get out of bed, get a glass of water, converse with my husband, connect with my son, and engage with our dog. Life was a struggle, and even the simplest daily routines wore me out. I felt useless, helpless, and hopeless.

Yet, her words, "It won't be long," brought me comfort and hope. It sparked curiosity. I could get through that day knowing it wouldn't be long.

Jesus shared this with his disciples in John 16 to let them know their grief would turn to joy. Just as he prepared his disciples for the pain of separation with the promise of reunion, Bev's words reminded me that our suffering is temporary and joy will come. "In a little while you will see me no more, and then after a little while you will see me." The impact of these words and the timing of Jesus' message are powerful. These words were spoken by Jesus while in the upper room, after washing the disciples' feet and giving his final messages before being betrayed and arrested. "Then after a little while you will see me" is similar to "it won't be long."

It's been over eight years since Jesus shared this personal message through my friend. One he gave her to share with me in the most painful time of my life. Over the days, weeks, months, and years, as I fervently sought the Lord each morning and cried out to him many times a day, I gained strength, hope and joy. I'm ready to meet him face to face any time. And, while I wait, I trust in his strength and faithfulness to help me live every day to its fullest, being wholly alive, bringing Jesus joy and honor in all I do.

PRAYER

Thank you, Jesus, for the truth of your Word and the hope you bring, even in the darkest times. I'm grateful for the jewels of truth you give others to share with me and give me hope and comfort. May I be a vessel through which you share jewels to encourage, comfort, and give hope to others. In your precious name, Amen.

UNLEASH YOUR PEN

Think of someone you know who is hurting or struggling in some way. Bring them before the Lord, pray for them, and ask the Lord for a word to pray or an encouragement for them. Be open to God's leading to share with others as he opens the door to do so.

Lori Waite Whitaker

Lori is the mom of a college-aged daughter. Born and raised near Detroit, she lived for several years in South Florida before spending most of her life living outside Chicago. She now lives in South Carolina, where she is building a new life. While relationships with some family members had sometimes been wrought with estrangement, her friends have been a life-long source of support, encouragement, fun, and love. For many years she worked in operations with an accounting degree until feeling prompted by God to pursue more of a calling and a desire to serve. Today she supports and mentors others as a spiritual director, Christian life coach, and Immanuel prayer guide. She also serves as a Journey Group leader, facilitating relational skills to help build healthy communities of individuals.

While journaling for some is a passion, for Lori it is an opportunity to write her thoughts and feelings. What began as a voice for herself led into love letters to God. It was the safest place for her to be her true self and share gratitude for all God's goodness in her life.

You can contact Lori at lorijwaite@yahoo.com.

Faithfulness

What if some were unfaithful? Does their faithlessness nullify the faithfulness of God?

— ROMANS 3:3 (ESV)

When asked about one's faith, the question may revolve around which church denomination one attends. Faith may be considered a form of loyalty. Yet, the question often revolves around how one feels about God or religion. It is a question some ask, and some only ponder.

There are times in life when many of us want to give up, throw in the towel, or any of the countless other clichés. I experienced a difficult time in life when I questioned how I was going to make it through. I learned to rely on God in ways I never had before, knowing that he was the only one who knew all the circumstances. I had to trust that he knew the outcome.

In reviewing scripture, I recalled that there was a spiritual battle beyond what I could do. Many Bible verses refer to waiting on the Lord, saying, "Do not fear" or "Fear not." It was crucial to let go of my need for control. I needed to deepen my trust in God. My faith was stretched, even tested, as I had to release more of myself and rely on God for peace.

As I found myself in that difficult time of tested faith, I felt compelled to draw inward. It wasn't a selfish choice but rather a realization that I couldn't make it on my own. The circumstances were relational, so I had no control over the other person, and the relationship had not always been smooth. What choice did I have? What could I do when I could not control the circumstances? Challenging situations arise for all of us in many forms; they may be spiritual, emotional, mental, physical, financial, or relational.

In my particular experience, I was surprised that there was much goodness happening in my life simultaneously with the trials. I had completed a long-awaited move to a warmer climate, began working in a field to which I felt called, and met a special person with whom to share life. Yet, never had I so clearly recognized the reality of an enemy, an adversary. The truth is that there is an enemy, Satan, the same enemy of God. I was left with no choice but to remind myself that the battle is the Lord's, as is written throughout scripture.

I was desperate to rely on God for what I needed in this particular difficulty. I had to have faith and trust God. I did all I could to stay connected to the Lord. There was nothing wiser or more practical I could do, and certainly nothing anyone else could do for me, to bring about resolution. Relying on God was the only choice that seemed available and was unlike other choices I had made throughout my lifetime. It wasn't an easy choice, but it was the only choice. I held on with all I had and, as a result, deepened my faith as I came out on the other side.

Later, a friend commented on my faithfulness. I could only reply that it wasn't my faithfulness but rather God's faithfulness toward me. It was he who carried me through. In my imperfect humanity, I certainly would have failed. God provided the strength and the direction. The Lord was the one who remained faithful. He deserves all the glory.

PRAYER

Lord Jesus, thank you that you do not want me to fail by relying on myself. Praise your Holy Spirit for bringing the guidance I need when I cannot handle life on my own. I know you see the entirety from beginning to end and want the best for your glory. Help me to seek you first in all I do. In Jesus' name, Amen!

UNLEASH YOUR PEN

Write about a time when you relied on God.

Grieving a Lost Relationship

> Grieving, yet always rejoicing; as poor, yet enriching many; as having nothing, yet possessing everything.
>
> — 2 CORINTHIANS 6:10 (CSB)

Relationships can bring hardship and difficulties. I grew up believing that my mother was crazy, certainly a result of my immaturity and lack of understanding. She suffered from mental illness. We struggled to find common ground on which to establish a relationship. As an adult, I have recognized how others' expectations of me were not always the best. When my mother attempted one such expectation, and I refused to oblige, she ended our relationship.

The absence of a relationship with my mother has been a tough path, difficult for most to grasp. Why couldn't I just forgive and forget? The well-intentioned suggestions of others prove difficult in bringing peace or relational resolve. God prompted me to eventually write my mother a letter, forgiving her and asking for her to forgive any hurt I caused her. One day, I received her written response.

She didn't share my beliefs.

I tried to offer forgiveness. My mom answered the few calls I made over the years, the conversations were brief and shallow. Each subsequent Christmas, I sent a card and a Christmas letter. I initiated all communication. She made no attempt to contact me. It was left up to me to determine how to resolve the fractured relationship. I received support from friends and counselors, and comfort and guidance from the Lord. Though forgiveness came, the pain lingered, allowing me to grieve the relationship. While I may not have had the relationship I wanted with my mother, I possessed everything in knowing my heavenly Father cared for me.

One year, I was surprised to receive a birthday card from my mother, realizing it was the one and only communication from her in decades. I was relieved and rejoiced in the forgiveness God offered to both of us, and I accepted that she found some resolution with me. There was relief in the surprise, like a gift, and a release of guilt for any hardship I had caused her.

Months later, my mother died. I felt a level of sadness in realizing there was never going to be a complete resolution for our relationship. Her wishes upon death were to have no service or celebration. There was no opportunity to gather with those who knew her in order to acknowledge her life and the impact she may have had upon others. Her body was gone, her life ended. Deep emotions swirled. I was disheartened that my lack of understanding to my mother's mental illness kept me from considering any suffering she must have felt during her lifetime.

The only thing left was to accept and honor her decisions after she passed. I was able to share grief and love individually with family and friends. I spent decades grieving the relationship. Suddenly, I found myself grieving my mother's life. Her passing emphasized the complexities of relationships and how easy it is to overlook the myriad emotions shared between two people.

Our lives become a testimony to God's work. We glorify God when others see our rejoicing, even in grief. Each story and experience, no matter how difficult, enriches others when we remain steadfast in the knowledge that the Lord is in control. Regardless of what we have in life or relationships, it is nothing compared to the relationship we can have with our heavenly Father.

PRAYER

Father God, please be with me when I struggle. Let me not stumble or pass blame. Although you have made known to me that I will have troubles and difficulties in life and relationships, thank you for never leaving or forsaking me. Help me to not forsake others but rather love them as you see them. In Jesus' name, Amen!

UNLEASH YOUR PEN

Consider a relationship you treasure and create a list of emotions you can share with that person. Consider how you may use your pen to process emotions in a difficult relationship.

Jesus Is My Rocking Chair

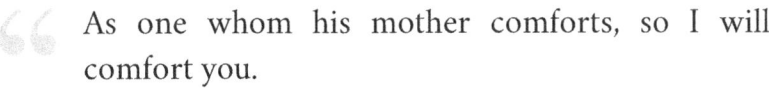

> As one whom his mother comforts, so I will comfort you.

> — ISAIAH 66:13A (ESV)

There are days when we experience uncertainty. It draws our attention away from our ordinary routines and into a greater need for self-care. This occurred to me one day. I paused to pay closer attention to my need for God. Much of my discomfort stemmed from having moved away from my closest friends. In the past when life struggles occurred, I would reach out to those who held me up with affirmation and encouragement, sometimes including a physical hug.

During a time of distress, I found myself in solitude, comforted in the quiet, as I shared my thoughts with the Lord. Then I called a friend in the city from where I had moved. As the call ended, I realized I sat in a rocking chair. It provided comfort. Then came a second day and another phone call with a friend who previously lived nearby. It was so good to hear her voice, to feel heard through affirmation. Although we lived in different locations, I was struck by the realization that, once again, I sought solace in a rocking chair. I discovered that a rocking chair helps during a time of frustration in life. There's something soothing about the rocking motion, reminding me of how babies are comforted when a mother rocks them to sleep.

I found myself considering cradles, bouncy seats, and rocking chairs of all sizes, designed with the purpose of comforting babies. I questioned why adults do not provide themselves with the same care? I continued rocking, feeling that Jesus became my rocking chair. As I allowed my heart to experience the love of God in the rocker, thoughts expanded to the arms of the chair. Much like how adults rock a baby in their arms, I felt held and rocked in the caring arms of Jesus. I smiled as he comforted me. I appreciated the rocking, like a baby being comforted. It was a precious thought to be so loved and cared for.

The experience of Jesus as my rocking chair continued to stay with me, even making me smile as I *sat* with the thought. I pondered that, whether in the ordinary routines or dilemmas of life, there remains great comfort in turning to Jesus to surrender all my cares. God provided all strength and hope, regardless of the people who may or may not be available to me when I feel a need to be seen or heard. The Lord knows all of it, and rocks me as I am comforted.

PRAYER

Father God, thank you for always being available to me. I often turn to you as my rock or my comforter. Thank you for reminding me that something as simple as a rocking chair can draw me to you. In Jesus' name, Amen!

UNLEASH YOUR PEN

Write about a time when you experienced great comfort, including details of what the experience was like for you or how Jesus may have brought the comfort.

Overwhelmed in Prayer

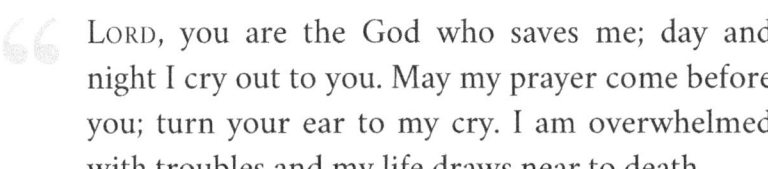

> LORD, you are the God who saves me; day and night I cry out to you. May my prayer come before you; turn your ear to my cry. I am overwhelmed with troubles and my life draws near to death.
>
> — PSALM 88:1-3 (NIV)

In my early years walking with the Lord, there were times when it felt like he brought a particular word to mind for me. He helped me discern words of light as opposed to words of darkness—words representing the Lord rather than words representing evil. As my relationship with Jesus became more intimate and secure, the words came less frequently.

Until recently…

While with a group of others, the word *desperate* hit my spirit with great intensity. I jotted down the word and a corresponding sentence so I could review it later in my devotional time. When I asked Jesus about the word *desperate*, it became clear I sought a community providing a sense of belonging.

As I pondered the word *desperate* and turned to Jesus for answers, instead of the word representing a feeling of hopelessness, it became an answer to what I needed, an answer to prayer. My family of origin had not been one of love and encouragement but rather one of sarcasm and unhealthy expectations. I grew up feeling like an outsider, desiring to be accepted. The meaning of simple words can differ greatly depending on interpretation, potentially causing harm or misunderstanding. My initial worry was my desperation, so it's easy to feel hopeless. However, I wasn't. I desired something God intends for all of us to have. In my case, it was a desperate desire to belong.

I felt a need to open up to all God had for me. I recognized a trust in who he is and an understanding that he truly wants good for my life (Romans 8:28). Over the years as my trust had grown, I had learned to listen to him.

We use many words in prayer, and we often only use prayer when life is filled with troubles or when we become overwhelmed. Regardless of what we cry or what words we use, the Lord turns his ear toward us. Be encouraged that the God who saves is the one who hears and brings the clarity or answers to whatever we bring to him in prayer.

PRAYER

Dear Heavenly Father, thank you for words that come alive. It amazes me that you desire all things for my good and that you turn your ear to all my cries. Lord, help me do my part in sharing words that encourage others to turn their eyes and ears to you. May they all see your goodness. In Jesus' name, Amen!

UNLEASH YOUR PEN

Listen to whether God has a word that comes alive to you today and write about it.

Embraced by Jesus

 Guard your heart above all else, for it is the source of life. Carefully consider the path for your feet, and all your ways will be established.

— PROVERBS 4:23, 26 (CSB)

Sometimes I forget how a few minutes of solitude fill me with God's goodness. A recent trip to the beach reminded me of how much I love feeling the warmth of the sun on my skin and listening to the movement of the water. The view of the sea offers various hues of greens and blues. My eyes observed the shade of the blue sky. I watched the movement of the clouds as they brought a sense of peace. A glimpse of heaven appeared as the sun's rays peered through the clouds.

I felt the contrast between the heat of dry sand and the coolness of the wet. I buried my feet in the hot sand, letting them feel the coolness underneath. I marveled at how God created the two opposing sensations from one source. As I walked the beach, I was astonished that there were places where the sand was firm enough to hold the weight of my body, while other spots caused me to sink deep. My thoughts swirled as I experienced the different textures and temperatures.

My awareness shifted to peace as I pondered how a few minutes on a beach walk brought thoughts of God's goodness and his creation. The song, *God, You're So Good*, by Kristian Stanfill played in my mind as tears filled my eyes. I was relieved; I no longer doubted God's goodness. It felt as though my intimacy with him deepened, yet his love for me never changed. It's me who has changed, becoming more aware of his goodness. Peace settled into my body and relaxed my shoulders. Again, I felt the sand under my feet.

My attention turned to feel my heartbeat, noticing its rhythm, much like the waves upon the shore. My vacation was adventurous, but the beach walk was a solitary experience. The vacillation between the excitement of activity and the quiet solitude met a need for balance that I often overlook.

I returned to the place where I started my walk and laid down my towel to rest. Again, I felt the sand under my feet, listened to the water, and watched the movement of the clouds. As I sat with curiosity, I sensed Jesus watching me. He is delighted to watch me enjoy his creation. He reached his hand to help me to my feet. He held me in an embrace that reassured me that I am safe in his arms. I pictured laying my head on his chest as if listening to his heart. He held me in a simple, life-giving embrace. He knows my needs.

My imagination blended my present body into my memory and I remained wrapped in his embrace. I want to stay in his arms forever. Tears from feeling overwhelmed stopped as I simply held his gaze. The tears often come from sensing the Lord's goodness and love for me. Yet, held in his arms, there is peace, safety, and security. These are new feelings, yet they feel familiar. God's love washes over me, and I'm encouraged to release my life to him. He frees me from my past and from all my tears.

God knows me.

God loves me.

I trust, and I believe.

I want to stay in Jesus' embrace forever.

PRAYER

Lord, I thank you for solitude and transformation. You are my rock, my refuge, my strong tower. You are the unending sand of the beach, the warmth of the sun, the movement of the clouds, and the power of the water. I am in awe of your creation, sometimes feeling as if you made it just for me. Lord, thank you for helping me see the beauty in your creation and your people. In Jesus' name, Amen.

UNLEASH YOUR PEN

Consider a time and place where you felt peace. Spend three minutes focusing on the feeling of peace and any sense of gratitude. Recognize God's presence with you. Ask him to help you see.

God's Movement in Stillness

 Be still, and know that I am God; I will be exalted among the nations, I will be exalted in the earth. The LORD Almighty is with us; the God of Jacob is our fortress.

— PSALM 46:10-11 (NIV)

There is something deeply invitational about being still and experiencing the nature and movement of God. While standing in front of Michigan's *Munising Falls* for several minutes, it was amazing to observe the 50-foot flow of water as the spring thaw rushed over the wall of the sandstone valley. As the image of the extraordinary waterfall penetrated my thoughts, my eyes closed to listen to the sound of the water crashing to the valley floor making its descent to a creek below.

Taking in the view of the mighty waterfall, I glanced throughout the valley, and noticed the layers of sandstone created over time, imagining the fossils between each layer. There were warning signs to keep a safe distance. The power of the water created an impression in my mind, utilizing all of my senses, beginning with the image of the swirling water over rocks and fallen trees, spotting the tones of red from iron in the rocks. The invitation prompted me to close my eyes and listen to roaring water. I heard splashing against the valley floor, the creek meandering as it careened over the rocks. Each sound ignited my imagination to engage with water surrounding each fallen tree, the flow change with each obstacle, and the islands of sand along the rapid water's path.

The cool, fragrant dampness of the air heightened my senses as I breathed it in through my nostrils. I inhaled the air, its temperature vacillating between the warmth of the 70-degree day and the cool dampness of the mist.

In stillness, we see how God designed the beauty of nature, inviting us to experience it with all our senses. As I stood in this awe-inspiring glimpse of a fragment of his creation, I wondered what else he offered? Was the invitation to help me notice nature, or something deeper and more spiritual? Thinking of nature's power reminds me of Jesus questioning the apostles' faith during the storm in Luke 8:25. He invited them to be still, just as he invites us, to be still—to trust him when there is movement or power, whether in nature or in life's complications. Be still, know, trust, and practice being still while God moves in your life.

PRAYER

Dear Heavenly Father, I thank you for the beauty of nature you have created all around me. Often, I see the beauty of nature in the quiet moments and, at times, in the power of your movement. Thank you for the senses you have given me to notice and experience all that is surrounding me. Please continue to help me see what you see, in all things and all people. In Jesus' name, Amen!

UNLEASH YOUR PEN

Be still and allow yourself to be aware of God's movement. Listen to what the Lord speaks to you in quiet. Write about what you notice about the stillness. If you find it difficult to be still, practice by sitting in quiet for two minutes and build up to longer periods of time.

Learning to Love Like Jesus

> This is my commandment, that you love one another as I have loved you. Greater love has no one than this, that someone lay down his life for his friends. You are my friends if you do what I command you.
>
> — JOHN 15:12-14 (ESV)

The King of kings, the Creator of the universe, knows me and calls me friend! Jesus considers me a friend, which astonishes me every time I read, think, or meditate on his words.

Jesus laid down his life for his friends. Pondering the sacrifice of giving my life for my friends, I want to show my unwavering support and dependability. Jesus *commanded* that we love one another. I want to be someone who loves as Jesus commands. How do I offer that kind of love? Friendship is worth desiring, yet the sacrifice may represent a great cost.

Jesus defines a friend as someone who lays down their life for their friends. I question my readiness to make that kind of sacrifice.

What is Jesus really commanding when he says that I am his friend if I do what he commands? The cost of developing and maintaining friendship includes time and effort. Friendship is something very precious in a life with little or no margin, given the demands of work, family, and even serving. Life often leaves me feeling exhausted and unable to sacrifice much for others.

There are certain qualities that make friendship worthwhile. Worldly relationships develop on mutual interactions or shared interests, while social media offers opportunities to have many *friends*. Christian relationships share a love for Jesus in addition to shared interactions and interests. I desire deep interpersonal relationships. While not always easy, I desire to be an authentic and vulnerable friend. I desire to offer loyalty and kindness to my friends. I want honest conversations where our hearts are joined and our souls are knit.

You cannot build trust with others without being yourself. While some may believe it is easier to present the *me* that I want others to *see* and *know*, we should strive to share our true selves. Any lack of authenticity limits what we can truly offer others in friendship. Jesus loves when we are open and authentic in our friendship with him. Besides, there is nothing to hide, as he already knows everything about us.

While Jesus commands us to love one another, he challenges us beyond what the world expects. Christians are commanded to love. In this passage, Jesus says to *love one another* as he loves us. He reminds us that he gave his life for his friends. Jesus always loves and calls us friend. He gave his life for the world.

There is nothing conditional or mutual about what Jesus has done. All I need to do is follow his example and accept the love and friendship he offers.

PRAYER

Father, help me be the kind of friend you call me to be. Teach me to recognize who my friends are and help me to understand how the relationships may be developed into more of what you command. Help me see all the benefits of friendship and remove any costs that prevent me from being a friend. I ask all this in the mighty name of Jesus. Amen!

UNLEASH YOUR PEN

Ponder and write about friendship. Who are your friends? What kind of friend are you to others? What qualities might Jesus see in your friendship with him?

Three in Community

> God said, "Let us make man in our image, after our likeness. And let them have dominion over the fish of the sea and over the birds of the heavens and over the livestock and over all the earth and over every creeping thing that creeps on the earth."
>
> — GENESIS 1:26 (ESV)

It is natural for believers to think of Father, Son, and Holy Spirit with any reference to the Holy Trinity. Thoughts deepen on the importance of community as God said, "Let *us* make man in *our* image, after *our* likeness [emphasis mine]." God didn't say, "*My* image;" he said, "*Our* image." From the very beginning of God's creation, we learn we were made for community.

The three in community concept stood out to me when I learned through gardening that many flowers, shrubs, and vegetables propagate more abundantly when planted in sets of three. Sometimes planting in sets of three is recommended for germinating or pollinating, and it is often suggested for appearance. Gardening often references rules of three. The number three is found throughout the world and in our lives. Did God intend for the number three to help reveal his creation in a new way?

Throughout scripture, we are taught to love God and to love others as ourselves. It can be a difficult balance to find the right amount of love for others and love for myself. It led me to ponder thoughts of community. Absence of love for God, others, and one's self may lead to actions perceived as evil or self-centered. And without God loving us first, how would we even know *true* love?

I was part of a recent conversation about how the first three fruits of the Spirit (love, joy, and peace) are foundational for creating connections with others. As I reflected on my own relationships, I realized that I'm drawn to individuals who emanate love, joy, and peace. It seems that these three fruits represent more of a true, authentic person. These are qualities I desire in myself and in those with whom I am in community.

Considering how community was initiated with three from the very beginning of creation, I continue to be curious and enthralled with its significance. In the article titled *What Does the Number 3 Signify in the Bible?* the author references the "profound symbolism of the number 3 in the Bible, which recurrently marks divine intervention, completeness, and spiritual significance." In the Hebrew language, "three, *shelosh(f) or sheloshah(m)*means harmony, new life, and completeness."[1]

References to three in the Bible are prevalent, whether it is Peter denying Jesus three times or Satan tempting Jesus three times in the wilderness. We can look at the importance of three when we consider that Jesus rose from death on the third day. We may also meditate on scripture, which reminds us that, when we are in heaven, we can anticipate hearing the awesome repetition of the three words, "Holy, holy, holy" is the Lord God almighty.

PRAYER

Dear Heavenly Father, help us see the variety of threes in nature, humanity, and the divine. Thank you that, from the beginning of creation, you provided evidence of how we are to live each day in community. In Jesus' name, Amen!

UNLEASH YOUR PEN

Begin to pay attention to the significance of three. Write about how it is represented in your own life.

Appendix

AN EXAMPLE OF WRITING PROMPT RESPONSES

To allow you to see how rich the writing group experience can be, we have each written our response to this sample writing prompt: "I saw God present today..." We each spent 10 to 15 minutes writing whatever came to us. No editing or critique. Just sharing our hearts with one another through our written words. Read below to see the variety of responses that can come from just one writing prompt. This is the beauty of a shared writing group experience.

LORI ANDERSON

 You have enclosed me behind and before, and laid your hand upon me.

— PSALM 139:5 (NASB)

I saw God present when...
I saw a summer sunset fade across my favorite lake
I felt a sharp winter wind sweep across my face
I tasted a handful of freshly picked wild blueberries
I smelled the first spring lilacs in bloom
I snuggled and rocked my grandbabies to sleep

I saw God present when...
I sang Christmas hymns with the gathered faithful at
my church
Family members shared poignant memories around a
summer evening campfire
My three-year-old granddaughter "read" me a bedtime
story, sang me a song and tucked me in
I found the perfect word to express an important
thought
My attention is drawn to the clock when it reflects my
birthdate

I saw God present when...
Last year's prayer journal reflected numerous answered
prayers
A friend's perfectly timed call delighted me
I discovered a special treasure to gift to a loved one
I reflected on God's goodness in ways I could not have
imagined at the time
I passed a stranger on the street, and our eyes met to
exchange a smile

ANNETTE BESEMAN

God's presence is everywhere

> *I see him in the majesty of the sunrise and the quiet of*
> *the sunset*
> *I see him in the sure transition from season to season*
> *I hear him in the voices lifted in unified praise at*
> *church*
> *I sense his presence as he sends people to encourage,*
> *comfort, and bring joy to my life*
> *I feel him as he guides and protects me throughout*
> *my day*
> *I feel his love as he reveals himself to me*
> *God's presence is everywhere*

JANELL GIESLER

Recently, during a haircut, my stylist said I had a bald spot on the top of my head. I followed up with a visit to dermatology and was diagnosed with alopecia areata. I was told this was most likely from stress, and I immediately felt more stressed to be going bald! The following morning, I made a long *to-do* list for the day. I remembered my *stress* problem and the recommendation to relax, so I turned to the scripture to start my day instead of my list.

God was inviting me to be with him, to find rest for my soul in his presence. The Bible verse in the scripture reading was from John 15:4 (CSB), "Remain in me and I in you." I considered what it meant to remain in Jesus and have him remain in me. I was struck with insight from God that I was a human doing, not a human being, and all my *doing* activities were fruitless without first being in Jesus and remaining there. My inclination when I considered this verse was to start a *to-do* list about how to be in and remain in God. Instead, I closed my eyes, focused on my breathing and opened my heart to receive his peace. Gratitude filled me for Jesus, Emmanuel, who called me to come to him and to remain in him.

I don't think these insights from God will eliminate the stress I feel in my life or cause my hair to grow back immediately. But God's invitation to be with him instead of doing is sufficient grace for all circumstances I will experience, even baldness.

DAWN ROGERS

I had a little tantrum this morning. During my time with the Lord, I felt the weight of a close family member's situation pressing heavily on my heart. With pen in hand, I journaled my thoughts and feelings, but the weight seemed to take over—I couldn't write. Overwhelmed, I poured my heart out to God, eventually finding myself on my knees, weeping. My tears turned to frustration and desperation as I felt utterly hopeless and helpless.

After my outpouring, I picked up a daily devotional, and the scripture for the day leaped off the page. Philippians 1:6 (NIV) was exactly what I needed. "Being confident of this, that he who began a good work in you will carry it on to completion until the day of Christ Jesus." I turned the verse into a prayer, inserting the person's name: "God, I am confident in this, that you who began a good work in [insert name] will carry it on to completion until the day of Christ Jesus. Amen."

In that moment, God met me through his Word. He tenderly rebooted my faith, affirming that he had heard my cries and knew my heart. His truth, my greatest love language, became my lifeline. I dried my tears, apologized for my tantrum, thanked him for his faithfulness, and embraced the peace that followed.

LORI WAITE WHITAKER

It is in the littlest moments when I feel the presence of the Lord. Recently struggling in conversations to connect with my daughter, the Lord brought to mind a piece of paper she gave me when she was a toddler. The visual recall of that green construction paper with foam star stickers brought such joy knowing that her words when she completed it at daycare were simply, "Show Mommy." The teacher shared the words when I arrived to pick up my daughter, and I wrote the words and date on that simple piece of paper.

While the physical paper is packed away after my recent move, I know it is somewhere. It serves as a visual reminder I could hold in my mind that God wanted me to remember a time when my daughter joyfully shared her artwork and excitement with me. God reminds me that just like he has struggled to get my attention and assure me that he loves me when I wasn't quite seeing it, the same may be happening between her and me.

I praise you, Lord, that you show up in the simplest way to remind me in the most ordinary spaces of my daily life that you are always with me!

Notes

12. SURRENDER IN STILLNESS

1. Warren W. Wiersbe, *The Warren Wiersbe Bible Commentary: Old Testament*, (David C. Cook Publishing, 2007), 929.
2. Blue Letter Bible, "Strong's H70503 - raphia," https://www.blueletterbible.org/lexicon/h7503/kjv/wlc/0-1/

   râphâh, raw-faw'; a primitive root; to slacken (in many applications, literal or figurative):—abate, cease, consume, draw (toward evening), fail, (be) faint, be (wax) feeble, forsake, idle, leave, let alone (go, down), (be) slack, stay, be still, be slothful, (be) weak(-en). See H7495.
3. Blue Letter Bible, "Strong's H3045 — yada," https://www.blueletterbible.org/lexicon/h3045/kjv/wlc/0-1/

   יָדַע yâda', yaw-dah'; a primitive root; to know (properly, to ascertain by seeing); used in a great variety of senses, figuratively, literally, euphemistically and inferentially (including observation, care, recognition; and causatively, instruction, designation, punishment, etc.):—acknowledge, acquaintance(-ted with), advise, answer, appoint, assuredly, be aware, (un-) awares, can(-not), certainly, comprehend, consider, × could they, cunning, declare, be diligent, (can, cause to) discern, discover, endued with, familiar friend, famous, feel, can have, be (ig-) norant, instruct, kinsfolk, kinsman, (cause to let, make) know, (come to give, have, take) knowledge, have (knowledge), (be, make, make to be, make self) known, be learned, lie by man, mark, perceive, privy to, × prognosticator, regard, have respect, skilful, shew, can (man of) skill, be sure, of a surety, teach, (can) tell, understand, have (understanding), × will be, wist, wit, wot.

14. GIVING THANKS WHEN IT'S HARD

1. Gilbert Keith Chesterton, *A Short History of England* (New York, New York: John Lane Company, J.J. Little & Ives Co., 1917) pg. 72

16. AN UNEXPECTED ANSWER

1. Ewan C. Goligher, MD, PhD, and Kyle Hackman, *Death and Dying: A Cate-chism for Christians*, (The Gospel Coalition, Canadian Edition September 13, 2023), https://tinyurl.com/death-and-dying, Accessed April 18, 2025
2. Goligher and Hackman, "Death and Dying"

17. THE HOPE CHEST OF YOUR HEART

1. Blue Letter Bible, "Search Term - hope," https://www.blueletterbible.org/search/search.cfm?Criteria=Hope&t=NIV#s=s_primary_0_1; Blue Letter Bible, "Strongs H8615 - tiqvâh," https://www.blueletterbible.org/lexicon/h8615/kjv/wlc/0-1/

   noun feminine cord (compare √ *at the beginning*); — construct הַשָׁנִי (תִּקְוַת, חוּט) Joshua 2:18, 21.

   noun feminine hope; — absolute ת Hosea 2:17 [Hosea 2:15] +; construct

19. WHO WILL GO FOR US?

1. Schutte, Daniel L. "Here I Am, Lord." Oregon Catholic Press, 1981. http://ocp.org/en-us/collections/dg/367/here-i-am-lord.

20. LOOKING TO JESUS

1. Helen H. Lemmel, *Turn Your Eyes Upon Jesus*, (Blue Letter Bible, Hymns Supplied Through the Gracious Generosity of the Cyber Hymnal Website) hhttps://www.blueletterbible.org/hymns/t/Turn_Your_Eyes_Upon_Jesus.cfm, accessed March 5, 2025.

22. BEAUTY IN GOD'S SIGHT

1. Merriam-Webster.com Dictionary, s.v. "beauty," accessed April 6, 2025, https://www.merriam-webster.com/dictionary/beauty.

31. PREPARE THE WAY

1. Blue Letter Bible, "Strong's H6960 - qâvâh," https://www.blueletterbible.org/lexicon/h6960/kjv/wlc/0-1/

קָוָה **qâvâh,** kaw-vaw'; a primitive root; to bind together (perhaps by twisting), i.e. collect; (figuratively) to expect:—gather (together), look, patiently, tarry, wait (for, on, upon).

40. THREE IN COMMUNITY

1. Hope Bolliner, *What Does the Number 3 Signify in the Bible?* (Crosswalk, Updated December 12, 2024), https://www.crosswalk.com/faith/bible-study/what-does-the-number-3-signify-in-the-bible.html, accessed April 13, 2025; K. Gallagher, *Hebrew Numbers 1-10,* (Grace in Torah, June 15, 2015), https://tinyurl.com/grace-in-torah, accessed April 13, 2025.

About the Publisher

Established in 1954, the Minnesota Christian Writers Guild has celebrated nearly 70 years of helping writers take their craft to the next level. Our membership includes beginning and professional writers, editors, and publishers who write for Christian and general markets.

The Minnesota Christian Writers Guild is a professional and educational nonprofit organization dedicated to serve professional and amateur writers by providing opportunities to exchange ideas, knowledge, and experience toward publishing works that reflect a Christian worldview. The Guild promotes the literary arts and provides opportunities for its members to serve the broader community. The Guild sponsors speakers, contests, workshops, and seminars that further our goals of instruction, inspiration, and fellowship.

Learn more about us at MNCHRISTIANWRITERS.COM

Check out this book...

Life is filled with reflections of our daily life. In the dry and cold moments of winter, we know spring is just around the corner, melting and thawing the snow for each new season of growth. Yet, those thawing moments feel so far away in the midst of trial and pain.

Seasons of Change is an anthology filled with stories of hope, redemption, and grace. Each author brings a unique and beautiful way to describe how Jesus holds us as we go through life's trials. There is a season of change coming, are you ready to take the plunge and experience the warmth of spring thaw the winter in your heart?

BUY ON AMAZON

Made in the USA
Monee, IL
27 May 2025

18243087R00115